SUBURBAN RAII OF TYNESIDE

Alan Young

Published by Martin Bairstow, 53 Kirklees Drive, Farsley, Leeds
Printed by Amadeus Press Ltd, Huddersfield, West Yorkshire

Introduction

I was born in Newcastle in 1951. Until 1955 Heaton was my local station, and it was where day-trips to the coast began. My earliest railway memories are of waiting under the Victorian ironwork that sheltered the platforms for the electric train to arrive, and of the calm being shattered by a main line train (steam, of course!) hurtling through the station on its way to Newcastle.

When my family moved to a new estate, Longbenton became our local station, allowing journeys on the northern half of the Coast Circle. Railway routes and station design, rather than the trains themselves, caught my imagination, and an interest in Ordnance Survey maps (to find out where the railways were) and geography grew out of this. Longer journeys by train, including the annual Ramblers' Excursion to Keswick, broadened my horizons.

The week before I started at George Stephenson Grammar School, Westmoor, my parents were trusting enough to allow me to buy an Area 20 Holiday Runabout Ticket giving freedom of travel between Berwick, Carlisle and Sunderland. By this means I discovered, among other interesting lines, the individual charm of the Riverside Branch. I had long known of the route's existence thanks to the maps in the electric trains, but it was quite an experience to travel on the familiar electrics on this strange line. The train seemed full of loud and burly men, most of whom smoked, and who left the train at a series of semi-derelict stations, until it was almost empty from St Peters to Newcastle Central. The scenery along the route was thoroughly industrial, with a succession of shipyards and foundries, and run-down housing closer to Newcastle. I discovered the disused Byker station; although I had often been taken shopping on Shields Road, I had not realised that this station lay concealed behind Beavan's Stores.

Thanks to the inexpensive N.E.Region Day Line Diesel Tickets, just as the 'Beeching axe' was at work, I was able to explore many other lines which were soon to close. Regrettably I took few photographs! It was some ten years later that I began making a photographic record of the Coast Circle and Riverside stations. I had visited the South Shields line in the 1960s, but my attempt to photograph its stations in 1972, before they were demolished, was a few weeks too late. In my determination not to let this happen again, I spent the next three years travelling the British Rail system to 'beat the bulldozer': very costly, but thoroughly enjoyable!

As a 'Geordie' I am proud of the Metro and of the way it has revolutionised travel on Tyneside. I cannot take any responsibility for it myself, but I remember, with amusement, writing in about 1967 to the appropriate member of Newcastle City Council suggesting that the local railways should be promoted like the London Underground and that the Ponteland Branch should be reopened! It was also gratifying to discover, as I visited the rest of the railway network, that no other minor railway could offer a greater variety of station designs than the Coast Circle, where my interest had begun.

The scope of this book is 'suburban railways, which correspond to the present extent of the Metro and its shorter branches. I extend my apologies to readers who search these pages in vain for a detailed study of the lines to Durham, Hexham, and Morpeth, or the Blyth and Newbiggin Branches!

Finally, my thanks to Nexus for recent Metro statistics and plans; J Alan Wells for valuable help; Martin Bairstow for encouraging me in this project; and to my wife, Sue, for her patience, interest, and help with proof-reading.

Alan Young

Southfield, Lancashire
May 1999

Carville still largely intact on 31 December 1972. *(Alan Young)*

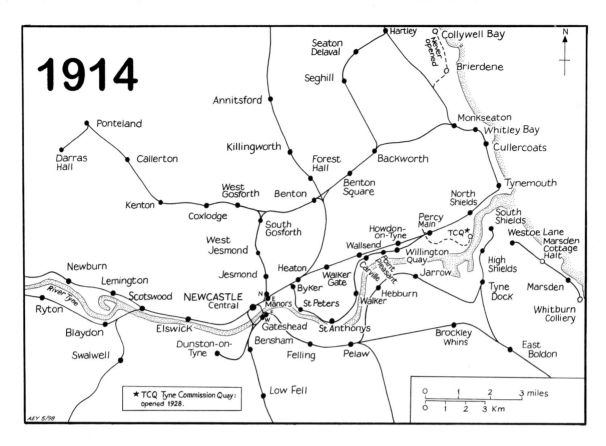

1914

Hartley
Collywell Bay
never opened
Brierdene
Seaton Delaval
Seghill
Annitsford
Monkseaton
Whitley Bay
Cullercoats
Ponteland
Killingworth
Backworth
Tynemouth
Darras Hall
Callerton
Forest Hall
North Shields
South Shields
Westoe Lane
Kenton
West Gosforth
Benton
Benton Square
Percy Main
TCQ ★
Marsden Cottage Halt
Coxlodge
South Gosforth
Howdon-on-Tyne
High Shields
West Jesmond
Wallsend
Willington Quay
Jarrow
Newburn
Jesmond
Heaton
Walker Gate
Carville
Point Pleasant
Tyne Dock
Marsden
Lemington
Scotswood
NEWCASTLE Central
N E
Byker
St Peters
Walker
Hebburn
Whitburn Colliery
Ryton
River Tyne
Manors
W
St Anthonys
Blaydon
Elswick
Gateshead
Brockley Whins
East Boldon
Swalwell
Dunston-on-Tyne
Bensham
Felling
Pelaw
Low Fell

★ TCQ Tyne Commission Quay: opened 1928.

0   1   2   3 miles
0   1   2   3 Km

N

AEY 5/98

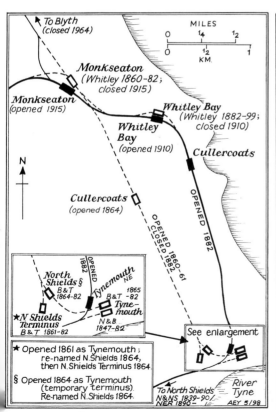

To Blyth (closed 1964)

MILES
0   1/4   1/2
0   1/2   1
KM.

Monkseaton (Whitley 1860-82; closed 1915)

Monkseaton (opened 1915)

Whitley Bay (Whitley 1882-99; closed 1910)

Whitley Bay (opened 1910)

Cullercoats

Cullercoats (opened 1864)

OPENED 1860-61
CLOSED 1882

OPENED 1882

N

North Shields §
B&T 1864-82

Tynemouth NE
OPENED 1882

1865
B&T -82

★ N Shields Terminus
B&T 1861-82

Tynemouth
N&B 1847-82

★ Opened 1861 as Tynemouth; re-named N.Shields 1864, then N.Shields Terminus 1864.

§ Opened 1864 as Tynemouth (temporary terminus). Re-named N.Shields 1864.

See enlargement

To North Shields
N&NS 1839-90/-
NER 1890-

River Tyne

AEY 5/98

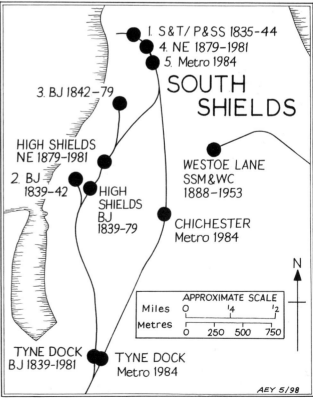

1. S&T/ P&SS 1835-44
4. NE 1879-1981
5. Metro 1984

3. BJ 1842-79

SOUTH SHIELDS

HIGH SHIELDS NE 1879-1981

2. BJ 1839-42

HIGH SHIELDS BJ 1839-79

WESTOE LANE SSM&WC 1888-1953

CHICHESTER Metro 1984

TYNE DOCK BJ 1839-1981

TYNE DOCK Metro 1984

APPROXIMATE SCALE
Miles   0   1/4   1/2
Metres   0   250   500   750

N

AEY 5/98

A journey around the Coast Circle

The suburban side of Newcastle Central on 6 May 1967 with electric units for the Coast in platforms 1 and 2. The class 101 diesel in platform 3 is for Alnwick. *(Trevor Ermel)*

The inspector at the entrance to platform 1 at Newcastle Central punches our Whitley Bay return tickets, and we are ready for a 1963 clockwise journey on the Coast Circle. The dark green two-car electric multiple unit is at the platform, its motor gently throbbing. To ensure that it is not an express service, a stroll to the front of the train confirms that it is 'Coast Stopping'. We board, after the customary struggle to open one of the sliding doors, and are greeted by the familiar sweet, musty smell of these 1937 carriages. The open saloon has ranks of 'bucket' seats with cold, brown, shiny surrounds. Bare bulbs project from the ceiling, and luggage racks stretch the length of the saloon. An outdated map of the North Tyneside electric system, still including Byker and St Anthonys, is framed above the door at the end of the carriage. It is accompanied by another familiar feature: the framed advertise-ment of a cavalier enjoying his McEwan's Ale!

The guard blows his whistle. Drawing out of the platform the train clatters over the intricate crossing, where the route to Gateshead and the south via High Level Bridge curves off to the right. The soot-blackened Castle Keep stands between the diverging railway routes. The YN& B Railway coveted this ancient building: its strategic position, overlooking the crossing and Central station, would have been

ideal for a signal box! The short distance to Manors is shared with the returning Coast Circle route and the East Coast main line. We are at roof-top level, crossing Dean Street by a magnificent arch (now a Grade II listed structure). To our left is the lantern tower of St Nicholas's Cathedral, its stone as black as the Castle Keep. A further bridge over the A1 road provides a fine view to our right of the arched Tyne Bridge.

At **Manors East** the two tracks and platforms of the Coast Circle via Wallsend curve off to the right, followed by the two tracks and platforms of the main line. We enter **Manors North** ($1/2$ mile from Central), its five platforms under glazed roofing. It is summer, and an array of hanging flower baskets decorates platforms 1 and 2. Passing under New Bridge Street the climb to Jesmond begins in a deep walled cutting, within which is Jesmond signal box. The concrete structure and sidings of New Bridge Street goods depot are to our right. To our left, and at first well above our level, are sidings on the site of the one-time **New Bridge Street** passenger station.

Having passed under Sandyford Road the gradient slackens as we enter **Jesmond** ($11/4$ miles). Although the line is below street level, Jesmond station is welcoming and well-maintained. There is clearly a keen gardener who tends the flower beds and can be justly proud of the Best Kept Station

The ticket barrier at the entrance to platforms 3 and 4 at Newcastle Central. *(Kevin Hudspith)*

certificates in the booking hall. Immediately north of the station we go under Jesmond Road, where the decorated metalwork of the bridge carries a B&T 1864 plate. The climb is resumed through a grassy cutting between sturdy terrace houses, then with its signal box to our left we enter **West Jesmond** (2 miles). This station is typically suburban, with red brick buildings, and awnings over each platform. Jesmond Picture House to our right, and nearby swimming baths, account for some of the passenger traffic here. The line continues uphill, in a shallow cutting. Shortly before South Gosforth, a rusty track branches off into the Craghall sidings, to be followed by further sidings and, to the right, its signal box. Like Jesmond, **South Gosforth** (3 miles) is a cheerful and attractive place. The platforms have colourful flower beds. The buildings, although grimy, are elegant. A typical NER iron footbridge links the two platforms.

Just beyond the bridge under Station Road, the Ponteland goods branch climbs and curves away sharply to the left. Our route turns sharply right, changing our direction of travel from north to east. To our right are cottages on Streatlem Terrace serving the long-closed Gosforth Colliery. From the left we are joined by a derelict mineral railway,

Interior of E29304E, 1937 electric stock.   *(Ian S. Carr)*

passing through wasteland. Soon the tall South Gosforth East signal box is reached. This controls access to Gosforth Car Sheds, also on our left, where electric and diesel multiple units are stabled. These sheds were built in 1923 replacing Heaton Shed which had been destroyed by fire in 1918.

Crossing over the Ouseburn and Salters Lane we have our first glimpse of countryside. Until the 1940s there were fields to our left for the next mile, but Longbenton housing estate now occupies them. On our right we pass a large gasholder and the Lucozade factory with its derelict siding, followed by **Longbenton** (3¾ miles). The LNER opened this station to serve Government offices (known locally as 'The Ministry') which sprawl to the east of the line but are largely hidden from our view by semi-detached houses. The journey continues past the site of **Long Benton** (4¼ miles), just beyond the bridge under Benton Lane. After some distance at ground level, with Longbenton estate still to our left and 1930s semis to our right, we enter **Benton** (4¾ miles). Like South Gosforth this station is attractive and its Victorian buildings are dignified. Once again an NER footbridge connects the platforms. Electric lamps are the only recent intrusion on the scene.

After crossing Station Road and passing Benton signal box, double track lines now curve away to the left and right to join the East Coast main line. We cross over the main line, and shortly afterwards an electrified double track route joins from the right at Benton East Junction. This is used by a few electric services which travel via Manors (East) and the main line on limited stop journeys to or from the Coast. Close to Benton East Junction is the site of the long-closed **Forest Hall** (not to be confused with the station on the main line). We continue north-eastwards, virtually straight and level, through waterlogged fields stretching away to distant housing. Traversing these fields is the course of Killingworth Waggonway, closed in 1942, which meets our route at Killingworth Crossing box. On the right are a siding which formerly joined the waggonway, and the waste heap of a disused colliery. Shortly afterwards Great Lime Road passes over us at the site of **Benton Square** (6 miles), closed in 1915. Our journey continues at a good pace, the driver taking advantage of this long, almost level stretch without stations. The course of Seaton Burn Waggonway, closed by 1953, crosses our route, identified by the bridge abutments.

A cutting leads into **Backworth** (7¼ miles), where Backworth Waggonway has a bridge over the station platforms. This station is on a tight curve. Its modest buildings suffice for the limited number of passengers who use this essentially rural station. After a bridge under another Station Road, the tracks of the Blyth and Newbiggin line climb away to the left, whilst our route curves right under a bridge carrying the former Blyth & Tyne route to Percy Main, followed by Earsdon Road bridge. Here terrace houses of Shiremoor crowd around the railway. Passing an inter-war housing estate and a short steep downhill gradient, the route continues into pleasant countryside. We rush past Earsdon Grange signal box, with a distant view of Earsdon village on a low hill to our left. Approaching **West Monkseaton** (9 miles) houses appear on both sides of the line, but at the station there is an uninterrupted view northwards across farmland.

Whitley Bay looking towards Monkseaton in 1972. This 1910 station remains substantially intact on the Metro.   *(Alan Young)*

A six car formation pauses at Tynemouth on its clockwise trip round the Coast Circle about 1947. *(W. H. Foster courtesy John Holroyd)*

This station, opened in 1933, is a charmless wooden structure.

Half-a-mile further on, the descent towards the coast continues. After two small over-bridges, houses enclose the route. At a tight curve we are joined on the left by the single-track Avenue Branch, used by diesel multiple units on the Blyth and Newbiggin line. A bridge under Marine Avenue leads into **Monkseaton** (9³/₄ miles). What a contrast to West Monkseaton! Dating from 1915, Monkseaton station is lavish, with wide platforms and large areas under high, glass canopies. The impression of spaciousness is helped by the two railway tracks parting company, with a lawn between them.

Beyond the station Victorian terraced houses draw alongside the railway on the left, but a wide area of sidings opens up on the right, where the original 'inland' route, closed in 1882, leaves us. The train scarcely has time to accelerate before a reverse curve brings us to **Whitley Bay** (10¹/₂ miles). We are greeted by magnificent flower-beds at this large, airy station, dominated by a clock-tower. The train almost empties here on summer weekends until early afternoon. Some passengers, bound for the beach but prepared to walk farther, have already alighted at Monkseaton. Connoisseurs of the more intimate Cullercoats Bay, who know that Cullercoats station is close indeed to the beach, will stay on the train until the next stop.

Whitley Bay is considered the mid-point of the Circle route, so we continue in the 'up' direction to Newcastle.

A short journey past Victorian and Edwardian terraces to our left, and more modern housing to our right leads into **Cullercoats** (11 miles). This is less spacious than the other coastal stations. On summer evenings, with crowds returning from the beach, the

platforms resemble those of Oxford Circus at rush hour. The journey continues southwards, with prosperous-looking houses to our right, and then, at last, the sea comes into view. Tynemouth Long Sands attract our attention, though St George's Church spire, and the isolated bulk of the Tynemouth Plaza, are also highlights. The brief seaside stretch is followed by our entry into the built-up area of Tynemouth, and into the architectural highlight of the journey: Tynemouth station.

Beside Tynemouth North signal box, sidings lead into bay platforms to our left, and two through lines are added between the tracks used by the stopping trains. **Tynemouth** (12¹/₄ miles) has wide platforms and a large area under glass awnings. Because the station is curved, the line of columns supporting the awnings is a wonderful sight. There is, however, an atmosphere of neglect. The station was intended to handle far more passengers than it does today. This impression grows as we depart past four bay platforms, one with empty coaches in it. Our route continues curving to the right. At Tynemouth South box there are sidings on the right, then we are joined on our left by the lines from Tynemouth Goods, the former terminus of the Newcastle & North Shields Railway. We are now travelling south-westwards and will continue in this direction to Newcastle.

After passing Northumberland Park to our right we enter a walled cutting, crossed at frequent intervals by small bridges, followed by the 786yd North Shields Tunnel, known as Tynemouth Tunnel until 1923. This tunnel had limited clearance, and in 1874 the NER obtained powers to open it out, but never did so. It was widened slightly in 1930. Prior to that trains were not permitted to pass within it because the up and down lines were too close.

The tunnel leads directly into **North Shields** (13¹/₄ miles), a cavernous place under a trainshed, so dark that it is difficult to tell where the tunnel ends and the station begins. It is a depressing scene, but it must have been worse before electrification when smoke lingered in the tunnel and above the platforms. It is a relief to continue the journey in daylight, past the Collingwood View playing field, Smith's Park, and the Ridges inter-war council estate, before crossing a bridge over a goods line and reaching **Percy Main** (14½ miles). This station is bleak, perched on an embankment. There is a cluster of terraced houses to the left, built for the former Percy Main Colliery, and a muddled landscape of railway lines, factories and flats to the right. Just beyond the station a trailing junction to our right connects with the old Blyth & Tyne route to Backworth. This is also used by Tyne Commission Quay trains. These boat trains travel via Wallsend, reversing once they reach the Quay lines, so there is a delay while the locomotive runs round the train. Passengers then enjoy a fascinating journey to the quay past the old Percy Main locomotive and waggon repair works, then through what seems an endless maze of sidings and junctions, travelling at a snail's pace – which explains why half an hour is allowed for the 8¼ miles from Newcastle.

At Percy Main West Junction the Riverside Branch leaves to the left. Between the two routes, as they diverge, is an expanse of derelict land. A level crossing at Howdon Lane – the only one across a public road on the Coast Circle route – precedes

Howdon-on-Tyne (15¼ miles). The site is dominated by the gasholders of Howdon Gasworks. The station buildings are unimpressive. Beyond Howdon our route continues straight ahead through more residential areas. Suddenly we are on the Willington Dene Viaduct, 82ft above the Wallsend Burn (or Willington Gut). The present structure of 1880, has seven arches and is 347yd long. Looking left we see the bridge on the Riverside Branch crossing the same valley. After Willington Dene the view to the left is of engineering works and shipyards, whilst terraced housing is to our right. Decelerating to approach Wallsend, we notice that the Riverside Branch has drawn alongside, with Carville station below us. It looks neglected, the nameboard too faded to be legible.

Crossing Station Road we enter **Wallsend** (17 miles), on an embankment, with buildings and canopies reminiscent of West Jesmond. This busy station serves the High Street's shops, Wallsend Shipyard, and densely populated Victorian terraces. The next mile is through more housing, mostly built since World War I, with a skew-bridge crossing Shields Road. A narrow north-south corridor of allotments and open land divides the housing areas. Stretching two miles from Walker to the Coast Road bridge on the East Coast main line, this space was probably reserved for a goods line to serve Walker Naval Yard.

After crossing over Benfield Road we enter **Walker Gate** (18 miles), with the extensive buildings

North Shields looking towards Tynemouth in 1959. The trainshed was removed in the mid 1960s.

(Stations UK)

Willington Dene Viaduct carries the railway 82 feet above Wallsend Burn.
(Alan Young)

A Metro Cammell diesel multiple unit arrives at Walker Gate on 2 January 1979. The footbridge is now at Pickering.
(Alan Young)

A similar dmu of class 101 is about to leave Heaton, platform 3, for the coast on 31 December 1972.
(Graham Larkbey)

An inbound Coast Circle stopping service calls at Manors East, platform 9 on 18 February 1967.

(Trevor Ermel)

of Walker Gate Hospital to our right. The massive structures of Parsons engineering works dominate the site, but the station itself is tidy, with an attractive timber building not unlike a sports pavilion. Leaving Walker Gate there are carriage sidings on both sides of the line, with Parsons works to our left, for the best part of a mile. On our right the old carriage works give way to the engine shed and complex of sidings at Heaton Junction, where the East Coast main line joins us. The double track main line remains separate from the Coast Circle.

The parallel tracks of the main line and the Coast Circle pass under Chillingham Road and Heaton Road, then through **Heaton** (19 miles). Sunk into a cutting with blackened retaining walls the station is gloomy, but its long canopies are well maintained and have recently been painted in the N.E. Region's favoured 'oriental blue'. A Deltic-hauled express heading for Edinburgh passes us, easing its way along the curving track serving platform 1. A few hundred yards beyond Heaton we pass Riverside Junction signal box on our left, where the Riverside Branch joins us. We notice the abandoned Byker station, still with nameboard stanchions and lamp posts, and the tunnel beyond. Leaving the cutting, an embankment takes us onto Ouseburn Viaduct. To our right is an unkempt, empty space where the Ouseburn valley has been landfilled and the river culverted. To the left, crossing the valley parallel to us is Byker Bridge. It is a 'classical' arched viaduct,

carrying road traffic, including the distinctive yellow Newcastle Corporation trolley-buses. Below and beyond Byker Bridge the dirty, tidal water of the Ouseburn reaches the Tyne amidst run-down factories and warehouses. Ouseburn Viaduct, over which we are travelling, is almost a twin of the Willington Dene Viaduct. Engineered by John and Benjamin Green, both were originally constructed in 1839. They each have seven spans and consist of segmental iron arches rising from stone piers, and were re-built to replace timber structures of similar appearance. Ouseburn (re-built 1860) is older and higher (108ft) but, at 306yd, is shorter than Willington Dene. The next half-mile to Manors East is through the unlovely Shieldfield area. The railway is in a stone-walled cutting, with bridges under Stoddart Street, New Bridge Street – which crosses obliquely so as to create a short tunnel – and Argyle Street. For the railway enthusiast the attraction here is the Quayside goods branch emerging from a tunnel at New Bridge Street. This is operated using an overhead electric 600v d.c. system (but with third-rail in the tunnel) and we glimpse one of the two locomotives of 1905 vintage. This goods service operates only as far as Manors East. After Argyle Street box we enter **Manors East** (20 miles), calling at platform 9. We re-join the route by which we left Newcastle, and return to Newcastle Central, after a journey of 20 miles 1166yd. Our 'Coast Stopping' tour has taken 58 minutes.

How the passenger routes developed

The Waggonway Heritage

Passenger railways in most of Britain had a 'clean slate' on which to be drawn. This was not so on Tyneside. As early as the 17th Century primitive railways, known as waggonways, were built in the Northumberland and Durham coalfield. Pits had been dug since medieval times but, during the 16th Century, Londoners began to discover the excellence of Newcastle coals. Growing demand for household coal encouraged enterprising landowners, large and small, to dig pits into the coal seams which lay a few feet underground. Over-land transport was simply not able to convey the coal to the capital, so it was moved by small coastal vessels.

The steep banks of the River Tyne downstream of Newcastle were rich in coal and close to water transport, so this was where 16th Century pits were dug. These early mines were sometimes short galleries, or 'drifts' into the hillside. Once these were exhausted, mining moved away from the river banks. Carrying coal to the boats became a problem, even though the journey was generally downhill, so one coal owner after another adopted the idea of guiding coal waggons to the riverside on wooden rails. Before rails were used, pack animals had carried the coals. The use of waggons was unwise because they caused ruts and potholes on the poorly-surfaced lanes and could grind to a halt in the mud. Canals, so useful elsewhere in Britain, were impractical because of the steepness of the valley sides. Where the waggonway reached the river, a staith would usually be built; this was a high wooden pile onto which the rails extended. When and where the first waggonway was used may never be known, but by 1608 there were waggonways from Beaumont's pits at Bebside, Bedlington, and Cowpen to the River Blyth, several miles north of the Tyne.

The routes of many Tyneside waggonways, therefore, ran from the pits to the River Tyne or, later, to the coast. Some threw off branches to further pits. By the dawn of the passenger railway age, which north-easterners proudly claim was in 1825 between Stockton and Darlington, there was a remarkably intricate mineral railway network in the Blyth-Tyne-Wear area. Wooden-rail waggonways were upgraded to iron railways generally between 1800 and 1830, and single 'chauldron' waggons were replaced by horse-drawn 'trains', though on some routes gravity and rope haulage were used. From the 1830s locomotives began to be adopted.

George Stephenson, born in Wylam in 1781, played a major role in locomotive development. While living at West Moor near Killingworth, he built his first engine, *Blucher,* in 1813. He went on to design and build 16 further locomotives and 39 stationary engines by 1825. After his work in the construction of the Hetton Colliery Railway near Sunderland (completed in 1822) he achieved lasting fame as engineer of the Stockton & Darlington, which opened on 27 September 1825 as the first steam-hauled public railway. Because the gauge of the wooden Killingworth Waggonway of 1806 was 4ft 8$\frac{1}{2}$in., Stephenson built his locomotives to this gauge; through his influence it was eventually adopted as the British standard. The cottage at Wylam, Stephenson's birthplace, still stands beside the trackbed of the former North Wylam railway. His home on Great Lime Road, West Moor, remains in use and is known as Dial Cottage.

When passenger services were introduced, some were on existing mineral railways. North of the Tyne, the Blyth & Tyne Railway from Hartley to Percy Main and to Dairy House (between Hartley and Monkseaton) used an existing route as did the Newcastle-North Shields from Heaton to Wallsend, and the original passenger line between Monkseaton and Tynemouth. The Tyne Commission Quay boat-trains likewise used long-established goods lines to approach the river. South of the Tyne the Springwell Waggonway (which became part of the Pontop & Jarrow Railway in 1853) provided a self-contained passenger service between Springwell and Jarrow from 1839 until 1872. Running almost parallel, the Stanhope & Tyne Railway (Pontop & South Shields from 1842-46) operated passenger trains from Washington to Brockley Whins, on the present Newcastle-Sunderland line, then on to Tyne Dock and South Shields. Another isolated passenger service operated on the South Shields, Marsden & Whitburn Colliery Railway. The remainder of the passenger network was on new routes.

The first route into Gateshead and Newcastle

The first passenger train service in industrial Tyneside was on the Newcastle & Carlisle Railway. From 1776 a series of plans for a canal had been proposed, and in 1808 Thomas Telford surveyed a Newcastle-Solway route. The first suggestion that a railway could connect the Tyne and Solway came from William Chapman in 1796. Then in 1800 William Thomas of Denton Hall, near Newcastle, proposed adaptation of existing waggonways for general and passenger traffic between Newcastle and Hexham. Finally the engineer Josias Jessop established that a railway could be built for a third the cost of a canal, and the route he proposed for the Newcastle & Carlisle received the Royal Assent on 22 May 1829. The line reached Derwenthaugh, on the south bank of the Tyne, on 11 June 1836, and was extended to Redheugh (Gateshead) on 1 March 1837. Newcastle passengers were ferried across the Tyne from Redheugh. On 21 May 1839 the Carlisle line opened its Newcastle (Shot Tower) terminus, replaced by Forth from 1 March 1847 until 1 January 1851, when trains were diverted to Central station.

Newcastle to North Shields and Tynemouth

A scheme to link Newcastle and North Shields by rail had come before Parliament in 1828. This Bill was rejected, as was a further attempt in 1833. A third effort resulted in an Act of Parliament on 21 June 1836, authorising a route from Pilgrim Street, Newcastle, to North Shields quay. A branch to Tynemouth was not approved. The prospect of a railway dismayed those who stood to lose business, including shopkeepers in North Shields, road coach operators, and boatmen. The Act protected coal traffic on existing waggonways.

Construction of the North Shields railway was by Robert Nicholson. Major engineering challenges along the route included the deeply incised valleys of the Pandon Burn, which was crossed by an 80ft embankment, and the Ouseburn and Willington Gut which were spanned by viaducts. Close to the Newcastle Carliol Square terminus was a 103yd tunnel, and at Heaton there was a 3/4-mile cutting.

The line opened on 20 June 1839. At first the rails were laid directly onto longitudinal wooden sleepers, secured together with wooden cross-bars. An early traveller noted that the rails gave 'an exceedingly smooth and equable' ride.

The intended Newcastle terminus at Pilgrim Street was never built, and the temporary Carliol Square station sufficed until 29 August 1850, when Central opened. From 1 July 1847 Carliol Square also provided a terminus for the Newcastle & Berwick Railway, which absorbed the Newcastle & North Shields in July 1846.

By an Act of June 1845 the North Shields railway was extended to Tynemouth, opening (under Newcastle & Berwick ownership) on 29 March 1847.

The East Coast Main Line

The so-called East Coast main line (ECML) first reached Newcastle in 1847 when the Newcastle & Berwick Railway entered, using the borrowed route of its predecessor, the Newcastle & North Shields. The ECML was primarily an inter-city line, but stations in addition to Central were provided at Manors, Heaton, Benton (later called Forest Hall) and Killingworth in the suburban area. A few 'slow' trains served these stations, their frequency changing over the years. Between 1904 and 1967 Coast electric expresses used the stretch from Heaton Junction to Benton Quarry as a short-cut to Monkseaton.

The Newcastle & Berwick Railway (later, York, Newcastle & Berwick) was backed by the 'Railway King' George Hudson, with support from George Stephenson. After gaining Royal Assent on 31 July 1845, Morpeth to Heaton opened on 1 March 1847, with the Tweedmouth to Newcastle (Carliol Square) service starting on 1 July 1847. The continuation of the ECML southwards was first by a temporary bridge over the Tyne carrying regular passenger traffic from 1 September 1848. This was reached by reversing the trains west of Manors just short of the incomplete Central station. The permanent High Level Bridge carried passenger traffic from 15 August 1849 and was formally opened on 28 September 1849 by Queen Victoria. Until 1906,

Class A4 4-6-2 No. 60028 'Walter K. Whigham' heads the southbound 'Elizabethan' (non-stop from Edinburgh to Kings Cross) through Manors East on 17 August 1959.

(G. M. Staddon/N. E. Stead Collection)

when King Edward Bridge was opened, ECML trains still reversed at Newcastle to continue their journey.

The handsome High Level Bridge was designed by Robert Stephenson, George's son. It was 446yd long and carried trains 112ft above high water. Five stone piers, sunk up to 40ft into the bed of the Tyne, carried six 125ft tied-arch spans, the outer ones being supported by the approach viaducts. The masonry was constructed by Rush & Lawton, and the ironwork (5,050 tons of it!) by Hawkes, Crawshay & Co. The special feature of this bridge was its dual-purpose nature, with the railway on the top deck, and a roadway between the arches below. Repairs and alterations have been necessary, including replacement of cast iron with wrought iron for the cross-girders carrying the rails (1893) and the timber road-carrying cross-girders with steel beams (1922). The bridge has been heavily used but is expected to give many more decades of service. It is listed Grade I by the Department of the Environment.

The Blyth & Tyne and the Coast Circle
Most of the passenger network north and north east of Newcastle was developed by the Blyth & Tyne Railway. On 1 June 1840 the Seghill Colliery owners opened a mineral railway in almost a straight line from their pit, two miles north west of Backworth, to the Tyne at Percy Main. From 28 August 1841 passengers were carried, and stations were opened at Seghill, Holywell (later re-named Backworth), Prospect Hill, and Percy Main. Until 1844 the passenger trains were rope-hauled. An observer in 1855 commented that this line was 'little better than a waggonway, carrying a few passengers in low-roofed, springless carriages, locally called "bumler boxes".' The section north from Backworth remained open for passenger traffic onward to Blyth and Newbiggin until 1964, but south of Backworth advertised passenger services ceased on 27 June 1864.

The Blyth & Tyne (the name was adopted in 1847) went on to construct the original Monkseaton to Tynemouth passenger line, following the course of the Whitley Waggonway of 1810. This was a continuation of its line from Blyth and Hartley, and it officially opened to passengers on 31 October 1860. The introduction of passenger trains was postponed until 1 April 1861 because the line had been damaged by landslips. The north end of this line from Blyth to Hartley and Dairy House had a short-lived passenger service, starting in 1847, which continued along a waggonway from Dairy House to Seaton Sluice. This service was withdrawn in 1852 when the Blyth & Tyne Act restricted passenger-carrying trains to the Blyth-Seghill-Percy Main line. The section of the B&T between Hartley and Monkseaton (called Whitley until 1882), known as the Avenue Branch, closed to passengers on 27 June 1864 when trains were diverted over the new route to Newcastle. The remainder of the line southwards to Tynemouth survived until 7 July 1882, when the NER replaced it with a line closer to the coast. Before its 1874 absorption into the NER, the B&T obtained authorisation in 1872 for such a diversion, but no progress was made, and the line which opened in 1882 was on a route authorised on 29 June 1875. The complex history of the Monkseaton/Tynemouth area is shown on a map based on the research of J.C. Dean. Details of openings, closings, and renamings are given in a later section.

The Newcastle to Monkseaton line via Benton (Benton station itself opened later) was the next addition to the Blyth & Tyne system. It followed an indirect route, going north for three miles to serve Gosforth, before swinging east and continuing north-east for some seven miles to Monkseaton (then called Whitley), where it met the 1860 Blyth to Tynemouth line. The Newcastle route was authorised on 28 June 1861, and construction began on 1 August 1862. No major engineering works were needed, other than a series of cuttings between the Newcastle terminus and South Gosforth (then called Gosforth). After a formal ceremony on 22 June 1864, passenger services started on 27 June. The opening of the Newcastle line allowed the original route via Prospect Hill to Percy Main and the Avenue Branch from Hartley to Monkseaton to close. The Newcastle terminus was at Picton House on New Bridge Street, about 300yd north of Manors on the York, Newcastle & Berwick Railway. The 'Coast' line was opened as double track from Newcastle through to Tynemouth.

The Riverside Branch
The Newcastle-North Shields line of 1839 provided a direct and efficient service, but the Tyne follows a meandering course between these points, and much industry and housing developed along its northern bank some distance from the railway. For this reason a riverside route between Manors and Percy Main was authorised on 13 July 1871 and opened to regular passenger services on 1 May 1879. The delay in opening reflected the scale of engineering works including Byker and Walker tunnels, a bridge over Willington Gut, lengthy cuttings, and substantial retaining walls. Although it was a loop, the new line was officially known as the Riverside 'Branch'.

The Circle is Electrified and Completed
The nonsense of having competing stations and unconnected lines in Tynemouth and North Shields was addressed by the NER (which had absorbed the Blyth & Tyne and the York, Newcastle & Berwick Railways). On 7 July 1882 a spacious new through station was opened at Tynemouth along with the coastal re-routing from Monkseaton. The almost circular journey from Newcastle to the coast and back, via Wallsend or the Riverside Branch could now be made.

By 1900 the North Tyneside system was almost complete. Electrification from Newcastle to Tynemouth included construction of curves at Benton South West (opened 1 May 1903) and South East (opened 1 July 1904) linking the ECML with the Coast Circle. The South West curve did not carry regular passenger traffic but gave greater

Trains of original electric stock, with clerestory roofs and matchboard panelling, pass at Backworth about 1910. The bridge carried the Backworth Waggonway over the NER.   *(Lens of Sutton)*

operational flexibility, whilst the South East curve allowed electric expresses to take a short-cut between Newcastle and Monkseaton. The Avenue Branch between Monkseaton and Hartley was re-opened to passengers in June 1904.

The short but invaluable line from the west end of Manors to a point a little north of New Bridge Street station was opened on 1 January 1909. This completed the Coast Circle, added a large station at Manors North, and allowed the New Bridge Street terminus to close.

The Ponteland and Darras Hall Branch

On 1 June 1905 the NER opened the seven-mile Gosforth & Ponteland Light Railway to passengers, leaving the Coast Circle at South Gosforth. Authorised in 1899, it was built as a single track with passing loops at stations. There were no significant engineering works. The Little Callerton Railway was authorised in 1908 as an extension to the Ponteland line, and it opened to passengers on 1 October 1913 to Darras Hall. Passenger services lasted only until 17 June 1929, but most of the route has been revived as part of the Metro Airport branch.

King Edward Bridge

On 1 October 1906 one of the last major additions to the national as well as the local network was opened. King Edward Bridge enabled ECML trains to pass through Newcastle without reversing, and increased the flexibility of train and light engine workings between Newcastle and Gateshead. Its

four tracks increased the number between Newcastle and Gateshead to seven. Associated trackwork created a triangular junction at the Gateshead end beside the engine works and shed, and a circular track layout including Newcastle Central and Gateshead (West). The designs for the bridge were by Charles Harrison, who was appointed Consulting Engineer to the NER Northern Division in 1889, and had prepared the drawings for the High Level Bridge. King Edward Bridge was 383yd long, and the rails were 112ft above high water. Three piers of Norwegian granite supported four lattice-beam spans containing 5,782 tons of steel. The northern span was 231ft long; the two central spans were 300ft; and the southern one, which widened at its southern end where the tracks diverge, was 191ft.

Late NER and LNER additions

From 1909 until the Metro revolutionised Tyneside transport in the 1980s there were few changes to the North Tyneside system. Minor diversions were made through Whitley Bay (1910) and Monkseaton (1915) in connection with new station construction. In Monkseaton's case, the new, larger station was to handle traffic on the Collywell Bay (Seaton Sluice) branch which was built, but never opened. On 15 June 1928 advertised services began over former goods lines from Percy Main to Tyne Commission Quay to carry passengers for the Norwegian steamers; since February 1900 unadvertised passenger trains had served the Quay, which, until 1920, was known as Albert Edward Dock.

In 1940 Benton North West curve was finally built. This had been authorised in 1902, and signals had been installed at Benton station in preparation for its construction. Under wartime conditions it was developed as a strategic diversionary route for ECML trains avoiding Heaton Junction and sidings which – correctly, as it turned out – were considered likely targets for enemy bombing. Until about 1949 and from 3 May 1971 until 1 May 1976 some advertised passenger services used the curve.

The North Tyneside Steam Railway
From 1991 there has been a revival of passenger services along part of the old Blyth & Tyne Backworth to Percy Main route (though not on the exact alignment) by the volunteer-run North Tyneside Steam Railway. A tourist service operates between the Stephenson Railway Museum at Middle Engine Lane and a platform a little south of Percy Main. There are plans to extend this line to the Royal Quays retail and leisure site, North Shields.

Pontop and Jarrow to South Shields
The earliest passenger service on the south bank was on the Pontop & South Shields Railway. Their mineral trains to South Shields began in 1834, and on 16 April 1835 a passenger service was introduced from South Shields, through Boldon to Washington.

Gateshead to South Shields via Brockley Whins
We have seen how the Newcastle & Carlisle Railway advanced via Derwenthaugh to Redheugh on 1 March 1837. From here the Brandling Junction Railway constructed a 1 in 23 incline, rope-worked by a stationary engine up to Greenesfield station, opened on 15 January 1839. The next section through Oakwellgate and on to Green Lane Junction (a little north east of Brockley Whins), opened to mineral traffic on 30 August 1839 and to passengers on 5 September 1839. At Green Lane the line from Gateshead met the Monkwearmouth to South Shields route which the Brandling Junction had opened a few weeks earlier, on 19 June 1839. From Tyne Dock, where the Brandling Junction built a station, their 1839 route swerved to the west of the Pontop & South Shields to serve High Shields, and a separate terminus station was constructed at South Shields.

Springwell & Jarrow Railway
This opened as a mineral railway, between Springwell Colliery and the bank of the Tyne at Jarrow on 17 January 1826. It was eventually extended further south west, but only the Springwell to Jarrow section carried passenger trains. This service was isolated from other passenger lines, though it crossed the Gateshead-Brockley Whins route. From 1852 the S&J became part of the Pontop & Jarrow Railway. Passenger trains ran from 19 June 1839 until 1 March 1872, when the NER opened a line following the Tyne from Pelaw to Tyne Dock.

The new route from Pelaw to Tyne Dock
The route now used by the Metro between Pelaw and Tyne Dock opened to passengers on 1 March 1872. There were no major obstacles except approaching Tyne Dock station, where a covered way took the railway under mineral lines branching off the Pontop & South Shields line to Tyne Dock itself. The 1872 line was valuable both as a passenger and goods route. It gave access to numerous industrial lines serving shipyards and factories in Hebburn and Jarrow.

South Shields, Marsden & Whitburn Colliery Railway
This mineral line was opened in 1879 from the NER Stanhope & Tyne route to Whitburn Colliery. From March 1885 passengers were carried unofficially between South Shields Westoe Lane and Whitburn. A public service commenced on 19 March 1888, surviving until 21 November 1953. The route was physically separate from any other passenger lines.

Tyne Dock Station looking towards Newcastle in 1959. Built in the 1880s, the buildings were demolished in 1972. The present Metro station is on a different site.
(Stations UK)

Steam on the Suburban Lines

A Clayton steam railcar at Morpeth on 18 August 1930 working the local service from Newcastle.
(LCGB – Ken Nunn Collection)

Before the coming of the local electric services, tank locomotives provided the motive power. Trains were hauled by 'A' class 2-4-2T engines dating from between 1886 and 1892, designed by William Worsdell and built at Gateshead, and 'O' class 0-4-4s built between 1894 and 1901. The rapid acceleration of the 'O' class made them suitable for the closely-spaced stations and steep gradients of the Coast Circle and Riverside routes. 'B' class 0-6-2T 'goods' engines, built between 1886 and 1890 at Darlington and Gateshead undertook passenger duties too, notably on the Blackhill and Consett routes. The older Fletcher 0-4-4 tanks dating from 1874 also operated on the local lines. Whilst some were converted into 0-6-0s for shunting duties, others were adopted as the engines for what were known as steam rail motors, rail motor cars, or – the term preferred by the NER – steam autocars. The 'A' class survived into LNER days as Class F8; 'O' class became Class G5; and the 'B' class became Class N8.

Steam Autocars
Increasing competition from road transport encouraged the railways to make their services more attractive. Thomas I. Allen, Line Superintendent of the Great Western Railway, is credited with the invention of 'rail motor cars', first used experimentally between Stonehouse and Stroud in Gloucestershire on 12 October 1903. Halts were also added at close intervals on this route serving line-side communities which had previously been missed.

The NER made little use of halts, but enthusiastically adopted rail motor cars, which they called steam autocars. The first service began between Hartlepool and West Hartlepool in 1905.

Autocars were push-and-pull units, capable of being driven from either end. They usually consisted of an elderly 0-4-4 Fletcher bogie tank passenger locomotive, with one or two clerestory bogie coaches. When two coaches were used the engine was coupled between the coaches. The end compartments of the coaches were modified to become driver's and luggage compartments. Circular porthole windows at the coach end were provided for the driver. The rest of the coach remained 3rd class, apart from one compartment which was redesignated 1st. The control gear of the autocars included a regulator, reverse and brake valves, and a speaking tube for communication between the driver and fireman.

On Tyneside, autocars operated the Ponteland service from its opening on 1 June 1905, and from 1906, Tynemouth-Blyth trains. They also operated from Newcastle to Sunderland and Durham, between Morpeth and Blyth (reversing at Newsham), and Morpeth and Newbiggin (reversing at Bedlington).

Steam Railcars
From 1925 the LNER sought to provide an updated version of the steam autocar, and in 1927 the steamcar entered service in the North East. This was a single unit containing the engine and passenger accommodation. Most of the fleet was of the Sentinel Cammell type. They took over the Ponteland/Darras Hall service shortly before its closure, as well as the North Wylam branch. There were also a few Clayton steamcars, with coupled wheels and external coal bunker, which operated from Central to Blackhill. From 1937 push-and-pulls were re-introduced with G5 locos. The steam railcars were all withdrawn by 1948.

Push-and-pull trains continued in the North East until the late 1950s. In 1958 the ancient ex-NER Class G5 0-4-4T engines still operated such a service between Sunderland and South Shields. The same locomotives worked to Blyth and Newbiggin until dmus ousted them in 1958.

The intricate diamond crossing and array of semaphore signals at the east end of Newcastle Central, about 1906
(Newcastle City Libraries)

67281, a push-pull fitted class G5 0-4-4 tank, is ready to depart Monkseaton for Blyth in the early 1950s.
(E. E. Smith/N. E. Stead Collection)

The Tyneside Electrics

Why electrify?

Newcastle suburban lines entered the 20th Century with steam-operated services. Competing road transport was provided by horse-drawn tramcars, which first appeared on the city streets in 1879, and by steam tramcars in Gateshead and Tynemouth. The NER's hourly service on the routes to Whitley Bay and Tynemouth, augmented at peak times, was sufficient to attract the public. However a transport revolution occurred when electric trams appeared in 1901 in Newcastle, Gateshead and Tynemouth, followed by Wallsend and North Shields (1902), and Jarrow and South Shields (1906). These were instantly successful, offering cheap, fast and frequent services. In Newcastle, where the trams were provided by the Corporation, the layout of the routes brought much of the city's population within five minutes' walk of a tram stop. Passengers deserted the railways: the 9.8 million passengers carried on the Newcastle-Coast lines in 1901 fell by about 40% to 5.9 million in 1903.

The Newcastle electric tram lines duplicated much of the railway route. In 1901 they opened through Byker, Heaton and Walker to Wallsend via Shields Road, and to Jesmond and Gosforth. In 1902 the ten-minutely Wallsend to North Shields trams of the Tyneside Tramway passed sufficiently close to Point Pleasant, Willington Quay, Howdon-on-Tyne, and Percy Main to abstract traffic from these stations. This company introduced a service between Wallsend and Gosforth (which lasted until 1930), part of the line following the defunct Kenton & Coxlodge Waggonway route. The alternative train journey involved a change of stations between New Bridge Street and Manors, or a long detour via the Coast. Again in 1901 electric trams of the Tynemouth & District Tramway began running between Tynemouth, Cullercoats and Whitley Bay. In two respects the trams did have disadvantages. First of all Newcastle and Tyneside systems did not agree on through-running until 1904, when Newcastle-North Shields trams began. Secondly the Newcastle and Tyneside systems were standard gauge, whilst the Tynemouth trams had 3' 6" gauge tracks, so no through Tynemouth/Whitley Bay service operated.

The NER took this competition seriously. The services of Charles H. Merz, a consulting electrical engineer, were sought, and with William McLennan he identified the benefits of electrifying the rail services and increasing the train frequency. Their report suggested that electric street trams were likely to carry short-haul traffic (under 2 miles) except where the origin or destination of trips were close to railway stations, but that the railway could develop suburban and inter-urban traffic if a more intensive service were provided. They believed that a frequent service throughout the day, such as the trams were offering, was crucial, since 70% of the population did

not have 'business hours', would not consult a timetable, and would not take kindly to waiting for trains. Peak-time passengers could be accommodated by increasing the number of coaches on trains. The consultants recognised the 'elasticity' of demand for travel; if trams could generate a tenfold increase in passengers – only 10% having been stolen from the railways – by improving the service, then the railways could do likewise.

The NER therefore decided 'to fight the devil with fire', and swiftly electrified most of the suburban system north of the Tyne. A third-rail 600v DC system was chosen for the passenger lines. Third-rail had been adopted successfully on the City & South London in 1890, and on the Mersey Railway which, on 3 May 1903, had opened the first electric line converted from steam traction. The dates of opening of the various sections of electrified track were:

29.3.1904	Newcastle (New Bridge Street) – Benton.
6.6.1904	Benton – Monkseaton.
21.6.1904	Monkseaton – Tynemouth.
1.7.1904	Newcastle Central – Tynemouth via Wallsend and via Riverside.
25.7.1904	Heaton – Benton East and West Junctions via East Coast main line.
5.6.1905	Manors – Quayside (goods only).
1.1.1909	New link between Newcastle and Jesmond via Manors North.

The Early Days of the Coast Electrics

Only nine months after electrification was approved, the trial run of an electric train took place on 27 September 1903 between Carville and Percy Main. On 29 March 1904, at 12.05p.m., a special train carrying the NER Chairman, Lord Ridley, accompanied by NER officials, left New Bridge Street for Benton. The first public service left New Bridge Street at 12.50p.m. the same day.

The electric stock was built at the NER York Carriage Works. The cars were 56ft long and 9ft wide, with matchboard sides, large windows separated by narrow pillars, and clerestory roofs. The entrances were protected by gates, soon to be replaced by doors. The cars had open saloons, rather than compartments as originally planned. The livery was scarlet and cream. The standard formation for the trains was three cars, as below:

Motor 1st class and Luggage	3rd class non-smoking	Motor 3rd class smoking
44 seats	68 seats	64 seats

Regular interval services on the fully-electrified system of 1904 were:

30-minute intervals:	Central – Monkseaton – New Bridge Street.
30-minute intervals:	Central – Monkseaton.
30-minute intervals:	New Bridge Street – Benton.
60-minute intervals:	Central – Riverside – Tynemouth.

To ensure that journeys were brisk, only a twenty-second stop at stations was allowed.

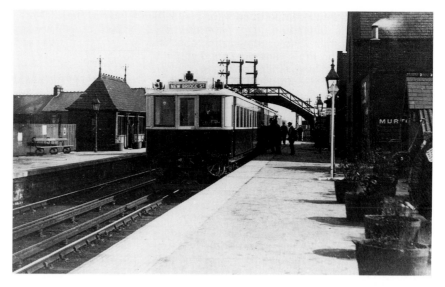

Benton Station in 1906 with an electric bound for New Bridge Street. The signal arms mounted with a cross (meaning out of use) had been installed for the north west curve which was not laid until 1940.

(Newcastle City Libraries)

Electricity was obtained from Newcastle upon Tyne Electric Supply Company, generated at Carville power station. Sub-stations were at Carville, Cullercoats, Benton, Pandon (Jesmond), and later Percy Main. A further sub-station, built at Fawdon in anticipation of the electric service to Ponteland, was never equipped.

The electrification boosted passenger numbers, so that the NER had to add cars to the fleet in 1909 and 1915. Growth was much slower than the decline had been, as these combined figures for the Coast and Riverside lines show:

Passengers carried:

1901	9,847,000
1903	5,887,000
1910	7,573,000
1913	10,192,000

The completion of the Circle route from Newcastle to Jesmond, with Manors (North) replacing New Bridge Street on 1 January 1909 made the service more attractive, but until 1917 the new link was used only by Central – Benton trains. As to profitability, K. Hoole estimates that running costs per train-mile more than halved, and that while total running costs increased by nearly 12% (owing to the greater frequency of trains) gross receipts increased by about 17%.

Although most passengers must have appreciated the fast and frequent electric service, the Cullercoats fishwives, who travelled into Newcastle with their baskets of fish, were now limited to three morning trains from North Shields via Wallsend. If they were bound for Jesmond they could use only one morning train and had to change at Backworth. The NER's reluctance to carry the fish baskets was explained by delays loading them into the trains and by the limited space for luggage in the new electric cars. Moreover, the water dripping from fish baskets flowed into 1st class compartments causing a smell that would offend the more discriminating passengers.

J. A. Wells in *The Blyth & Tyne Branch Part II* describes an additional electric train operation from NER to British Railways days on the North and South Tyneside lines, known by local railwaymen as the 'Control Set'. This name arose because it was at the disposal of Newcastle District Control for use as required in addition to its scheduled runs. In the early days a rake of ten six-wheeled coaches between two motor parcel vans was used chiefly to carry workmen to and from the shipyards. In 1929 six bogie coaches with compartments replaced the six-wheelers. The motor vans were replaced by the 1937 batch. The set operated until the mid-1950s before the coaches were towed to Ponteland for storage for some years prior to being scrapped.

Goods services on the Coast Circle and Riverside remained steam-hauled. Goods train movements beyond the limited electrified network would be impossible without a change of engine, and an electric live rail in yards and sidings was considered hazardous. Electric haulage of goods trains would therefore have needed overhead wires in sidings, and locomotives equipped for both third-rail and overhead current collection. Only the short Quayside branch was converted for electric goods operation.

The electric services suffered a setback on 11 August 1918 when fire at Walker Gate Carriage Sheds destroyed 34 cars. A replacement steam service was re-introduced to augment the surviving electric units. Between 1920 and 1922, 35 cars were built to replace what had been destroyed. Again, these were built at York, with electrical fittings by British Thomson-Houston. They had elliptical, rather than clerestory, roofs, and were delivered in self-coloured crimson lake. Some of this stock had motors (all-3rd or 1st-and-3rd class); some had driving compartments at both ends, and some at one end only. Trailer coaches were also constructed. At first the seats in the cars were reversible. Motor luggage vans were useful additions to the stock.

These contained large compartments for boxes of fish and parcels but could also haul ordinary vehicles such as milk vans or non-electric coaches for workmen's traffic. Pram vans were another of the new deliveries, containing limited numbers of seats. In 1923 the new Gosforth Car Sheds were commissioned to stable the electric fleet, with ten through lines and two into the repair shop. North of the sheds the construction of Gosforth Garden Village began in 1926 to house railway employees.

Under the LNER, electric stock began to be re-painted in teak livery, a change which does not seem to have been popular. For some time trains in each of the three liveries could be seen together on the Coast Circle.

North Tyneside Electrics from 1937-1967

Almost all of the existing electric passenger stock was replaced in 1937 with steel-bodied Metro-Cammell units. These operated until diesel multiple units took over in 1967. On 30 July 1937 the Lord Mayor of Newcastle launched the service of red and cream trains. Four years later they were re-painted in mid-blue and off-white. 64 twin-units and four single cars were delivered. At each end of the 55' 9" body-length were manually operated sliding doors. The new motor cars were rated at 216hp compared with 125hp of the 1904 stock.

K. Hoole's definitive work *The North Eastern Electrics* provides plentiful information on the Metro-Cammell and earlier rolling stock, but the following brief details on the 1937 cars may be of interest here. There were four types of twin-units:

12 of Type A	Motor single driver 3rd class	64 seats	
	Trailer single driver 3rd	64	Unit total: 128 seats
16 of Type B	Luggage Motor single driver 3rd	52	
	Trailer single driver 1st		
	28 1st + 32 convertible	112 seats	
18 of Type C	Motor single driver 3rd	64	
	Trailer non-driving 3rd	68	132 seats
18 of Type D	Trailer non-driving 1st		
	28 1st + 36 convertible		
	Luggage Motor single driver 3rd 52	116 seats	

Normal train formations were:

8-car formation	B+A+C+D	488 seats
6-car formation	B+C+D	360 seats
4-car formation	C+D	248 seats
2-car formation	A	128 seats

The new stock continued the tradition of open saloons rather than compartments, and they had distinctive bucket seats. Luggage racks stretched the length of the cars. Four of the 1920s cars were re-introduced between 1951 and 1955, converted into pram vans, with longitudinal wooden seats. They were used on summer Saturdays and Sundays and Bank Holidays, but were withdrawn in May 1960.

The 1937 stock reduced the Circle journey from 63 to 53 minutes. This was not changed after Longbenton station was added in 1947: instead one

The 1937 stock included two motor parcels vans, Nos.2424 and 2425 which could work singly or hauling other vans. Tynemouth, about 1947. *(W. Hubert Foster, courtesy John Holroyd)*

minute less was allowed on the West Jesmond-South Gosforth and Walker Gate-Heaton sections. Platforms were lengthened at Percy Main, Howdon-on-Tyne, and Walker Gate in preparation for 8-car trains. In a practice dating back to January 1920, a basic 20-minute interval weekday service was provided.

Passenger business thrived in the two years following the introduction of the new rolling stock, possibly reaching its highest-ever level on August Bank Holiday Monday 1939 when some 100,000 tickets were collected at the four coastal stations.

J. Joyce in *Roads and Rails of Tyne & Wear* gives interesting details of how the operations management coped from 1938 with the vagaries of summer Sunday traffic. Depending on the weather, and their experience, the District Superintendent and District Passenger Manager decided on Saturday which of three timetable models to adopt:

A   90 departures ex-Central using six 6-car and four 8-car trains;

B   Over 100 departures using seven 6-car and six 8-car trains;

C   Most intensive using twelve 6-car and five 8-car trains plus fifteen extras ex-Manors (North).

The management could also cope with unexpected homeward rushes: for instance an outward train via Wallsend could be stopped at Tynemouth to collect passengers and sent back the way it came.

British Railways assumed control of the electric lines on 1 January 1948 and changed the livery of the units to a light green (later replaced by a darker shade). They continued to give good service, but passenger use declined during the 1950s and into the 1960s. Figures for tickets issued in 1951 and 1967 show that the four coastal stations and those on the Heaton-North Shields stretch generally lost traffic, whilst from Manors to Benton there was a slight increase. No longer youthful, the trains were allowed a more leisurely journey around the Circle, increasing to 58 minutes in summer 1963.

By 1960, the North Tyne electrics were advertised as second class only which meant that anybody could ride in the former first class compartments.

Passenger bookings at Coast Circle stations

	1911	1951	1967	1972
Newcastle Cent.	3,054,004	2,538,865	2,159,321	4,658,850
Manors	no data	186,384	201,173	346,217
Jesmond	144,158	59,107	67,017	110,451
West Jesmond	112,440	84,650	113,813	151,354
South Gosforth	210,455	112,325	148,852	175,731
Longbenton	-	no data	175,164	286,016
Benton	177,003	121,847	148,515	170,473
Backworth	164,927	128,161	99,174	90,004
West Monkseaton	-	232,112	223,448	193,549
Monkseaton	241,313	524,486	387,572	319,435
Whitley Bay	509,974	475,798	368,789	386,444
Cullercoats	271,939	327,905	212,788	220,617
Tynemouth	356,303	201,953	182,858	253,169
North Shields	1,107,300	455,835	377,884	630,942
Percy Main	228,273	176,949	159,817	223,220
Howdon-on-Tyne	116,204	no data	211,722	269,556
Wallsend	322,763	212,953	259,466	397,734
Walker Gate	56,278	163,009	127,672	153,163
Heaton	519,350	262,640*	127,018	128,399

* Heaton 1951 figure includes tickets issued at Byker

A train of 1937 stock at Newcastle about 1947.

(*W. Hubert Foster, courtesy John Holroyd*)

A Newcastle bound electric unit at Benton, 1960s. *(N. E. Stead Collection)*

40071 at Tynemouth in the summer of 1978 about 4.30am with a single newspaper van which had arrived in Newcastle as part of the overnight newspaper train from Manchester. *(N.E. Stead)*

Diesel multiple units take over on North Tyneside

In December 1962 British Railways announced its intention of withdrawing the electric services. The Beeching Report of March 1963 did not earmark the Coast Circle for closure though the Riverside branch was listed. On a visit to Tyneside, Dr Beeching remarked that the closure of the Circle route remained a possibility. By the mid-1950s average receipts per passenger were 6d whilst direct costs were 7½d, and losses continued to increase. Eventually it was announced that the line would remain open, but that diesel multiple units would replace the electrics. It was claimed that the emus were life-expired and that, because of withdrawal of so many services around the country, there were dmus available which were suitable for the Coast line. It was claimed that losses would be reduced by more than a quarter, with diesel operation.

So the retrogressive step was taken of withdrawing the electric services. The last electric train left Central at 18.15 on 17 June 1967. Rakes of withdrawn emus were left at Heaton sidings before being scrapped at Blyth. A memento of the electrics appeared briefly at Manors: some of the familiar bucket seats were installed in the waiting room on platform 1.

Dmus had gradually been phased in over the previous year, cast-offs from elsewhere on the network. Their destination blinds showed such unlikely locations as Taunton and Yeovil Pen Mill,

and equally unhelpful route maps were displayed in the cars. A further six minutes was allowed for the Circle journey from 6 March 1967 increasing the time to 64 minutes. It was painfully clear that with closely-spaced stations the poor acceleration of the dmus made them unsuited to their task. Tynesiders even resented the loss of sliding doors to which they were accustomed on the emus, and the patronising notices about the dangers of misusing dmu slam-doors. A strange decision was taken to reduce the frequency of the off-peak all-stops service to half-hourly, with one fast train per hour in each direction calling only at Manors, stations from West Monkseaton to North Shields, Wallsend, and Manors again. The wisdom of Merz and McLennan in 1903 that passengers were attracted by frequent services and did not use timetables seemed to have been forgotten. Passenger loadings stagnated. Stations seemed neglected, particularly after dark when ageing lamps were often unlit. One positive side to the introduction of dmus was that, for the first time, passengers could have a view of the line ahead, which had not been possible in the electrics.

It is probably fair to conclude that de-electrification was a declaration of lack of faith in the future of the North Tyneside line. Contemporary BR thinking may well have been that the diesels would keep the service going until they, in turn, became life expired, at which time the line would close.

A Metro Cammell class 101 dmu pauses at Manors, platform 9 on the truncated route from West Monkseaton to Newcastle via Wallsend on 30 March 1978.   *(Alan Young)*

The arrival and departure of the South Shields electrics

Merz and McLennan were asked in 1908 to undertake a feasibility study into electrification from Newcastle to South Shields and Sunderland, and between South Shields and Sunderland. This would affect 21 route-miles, and 52½ track-miles, including sidings. It was calculated that a further 84 vehicles would be needed for the new services, and a new station was proposed at Fulwell between East Boldon and Monkwearmouth (Seaburn was eventually opened on 3 May 1937 in this vicinity).

World War I came and went, and no progress was made. The idea was revived in 1935, when an LNER Committee recommended that the Newcastle-South Shields service should be electrified. Apart from allowing a speeding up of the service from 34 to 27 minutes, operations at the east end of Newcastle Central would be eased without loco run-round and light-engine movements. No recommendation was made about electrification to Sunderland.

The Newcastle-South Shields steam-hauled passenger service was augmented in January 1910 to a twenty-minute interval on weekdays and thirty-minute on Sundays, taking 35 minutes for the all-stops journey. In the 1930s, before electrification was re-considered, diesel electric railcars were suggested for the South Shields service.

Electric trains commenced between Newcastle and South Shields on 14 March 1938. While the North Tyneside lines had brand-new 1937 stock, their cast-off 1920-22 stock was renovated and cascaded onto the South Shields run. In 1955 BR replaced these ageing vehicles with fifteen twin-sets, built at the Southern Region Eastleigh Works. The new units looked distinctly 'Southern'. They comprised a Luggage Motor 2nd, single driving, and a Trailing Composite, single driving. The motor car contained two 2nd saloons, whilst the trailer included a 2nd saloon, a 1st compartment, and four 2nd compartments. Whilst on North Tyneside passengers used the sliding end-doors, which could cause delays at stations stops, each 'bay' and compartment of the new South Shields stock had its own slam door. Compartments on Tyneside electrics were a novelty. An inconvenience of the new stock was the impossibility of moving between the two cars. To save the driver from changing ends, South Shields electrics reached the Gosforth Car Sheds via the main line and Benton South West Curve.

Passenger use of the South Shields line declined by some 50% between 1938 and 1962 when the weekday train frequency was reduced to thirty-minutes. As an economy measure the electric service was withdrawn on 7 January 1963, and within a few months the emus 'went home' to the Southern Region. The dmu journey time increased from 26 to 29 minutes. Winter Sunday services ceased from 1964.

A train of 1920 stock restarts from Pelaw, bound from South Shields to Newcastle about 1947.
(W. Hubert Foster, courtesy John Holroyd)

The Tynerider arrives

On 5 October 1970 British Rail Eastern Region (the North Eastern Region having been absorbed into its neighbour on 1 January 1967) embarked upon a campaign to revitalise the former electric lines. With a blaze of orange-coloured publicity, the 'Tynerider' promotion was launched. 'Tynesider – this is your line', proclaimed the first page of a free booklet. Inside, it went on: *'The Tyne coast railway is changing. It has become one of the most efficient and go-ahead local lines in Britain. That's because new ideas and new train services have been introduced. They're called Tynerider trains. Tynerider trains give a service that's specially developed for Tynesiders. The more you use them, the more they will offer you.'* In contrast to the sombre publication of 1967 reassuring the public that the dieselisation was not all bad, the Tynerider campaign was up-beat. The publicity booklet went on to introduce readers to Tommy Smith, a school-day Tynerider; Mrs Butterfield, an off-peak Tynerider; the nattily-dressed Charlie Barrett, an 'everyday' Tynerider; and Sid and Joy, the 'late-night Tyneriders', who used the new flat-rate 'all-night' service.

The 'Tynerider' promotion appeared to have a dramatic effect on passenger use, which increased by 60% in the North Tyneside area in the first two months (October-November 1970) but this coincided with a bus work-to-rule. December train loadings were 35% above pre-Tynerider figures. Passengers carried on the North Tyneside system rose from 7,800,000 in 1970 (including three 'Tynerider' months) to 8,480,000 in 1971. The twenty-minute interval service was restored, operating from 06.00 until 24.00, with an extra up-commuter express in the morning from Tynemouth calling at stations to West Monkseaton, then Manors, and a reverse working in the evening peak. An 'all-night' (Mondays excepted) service began, leaving Central at 01.15, 02.25, and 04.25 calling at all stations via Wallsend and Benton, except Manors. The stations were unstaffed when these trains called. Brightly coloured signs at the Central station above the entrances to the local platforms read 'Welcome to the Tynerider Trains', and the east end ticket office was renamed the 'Tynerider' office. Trains were adorned with transfers, giving them names of local folk-heroes such as 'Cushy Butterfield' and 'Harry Hotspur.' These customised units could not be confined to local lines, and appeared as far away as York and Harrogate, where a train named 'Cushy Butterfield' must have caused surprise!

There was a genuine improvement both to the image and to the off-peak frequency of trains at most stations on the Circle, but much remained unchanged. The same dmus still plodded round the route in 64 minutes; the South Shields service was virtually unchanged with its half-hour frequency retained; and the Riverside service was reduced. Most of the stations were soon re-lit and re-signed. On the South Shields line, the stations, with the exception of the terminus, had become unstaffed, and were not pleasant places to wait for trains. From Felling to High Shields the platform buildings were demolished in 1972 and replaced by small shelters.

The Tynerider initiative showed there was still life in the system. The growth in passenger traffic encouraged the recently-formed Tyneside Passenger Transport Executive, whose ambitious plans for a new Metropolitan Railway, incorporating the Coast Circle and South Shields lines, received the Royal Assent in 1973.

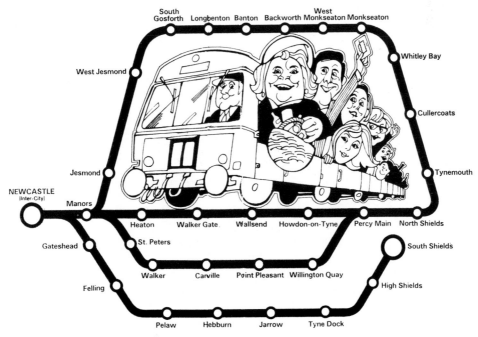

The 16.49 for Newcastle (direct) approaches Walker on 4 July 1973   *(Alan Young)*

The same train finds little business at St Peters.
(Alan Young)

Two class 105 Cravens units pass at the construction site of Four Lane Ends Metro Station on 5 April 1977.

(Alan Young)

Newcastle Central Station

Newcastle Central viewed from the Castle Keep on 30 December 1977.   *(Alan Young)*

The Newcastle & Carlisle Railway opened in stages between 9 March 1835 and 18 June 1838. The original eastern terminus serving Newcastle was at Redheugh in Gateshead (opened on 1 March 1837): passengers from Newcastle were ferried across the River Tyne by barge. Newcastle itself was reached on 21 May 1839, with a temporary station close to the Shot Tower, several hundred yards west of the present Central station. The line was extended to Forth on 1 March 1847, and the station at Shot Tower was closed.

Meanwhile the Newcastle & North Shields Railway reached central Newcastle on 20 June 1839. Its terminus at Carliol Square had a booking office and waiting room, with turntables at the end of each of its two tracks. This closed when services were extended to Central station, opened on 29 August 1850, which was shared with the York, Newcastle & Berwick Railway. Passengers who had benefited from the position of Carliol Square at the eastern end of the main business district were now served by Manors, opened on 1 July 1847. After closure, Carliol Square station building survived as offices until the 1930s.

The Newcastle & Carlisle Railway was finally extended into Central Station on 1 January 1851. Forth was closed to passengers, but the site served as Forth Banks goods station from 2 January 1854.

From 3 March 1871 it was renamed Forth goods station.

The Blyth & Tyne Railway entered Newcastle from the north, terminating at Picton House on the north side of New Bridge Street on 27 June 1864. This station was several hundred yards north of Manors. There was no rail connection with Manors until 1 January 1909, when New Bridge Street closed to passengers to be replaced by Manors North.

From 1909 Newcastle was fortunate in having one major city centre station. In London, Manchester, Birmingham, Glasgow, and many lesser towns and cities passengers had the inconvenience of changing stations to continue their journey, but at Newcastle this could be done within one station, sheltered from the elements, and with a porter to carry the luggage. The only minor inconvenience was the use of Manors North for terminating most Blyth and Newbiggin services, but there were frequent trains from Central to Manors North.

Central station, built for the York, Newcastle & Berwick Railway, was formally opened by Queen Victoria and Prince Albert on 29 August 1850. (The YN&B was absorbed into the North Eastern Railway in 1854). As one of the 'railway cathedrals' of Britain it enjoys Department of the Environment Grade II* status. This magnificent station was the work of the architect and landscape gardener, John Dobson,

Newcastle Central exterior and portico about 1910.
(Peter E Baughan collection)

The concourse at Newcastle Central in 1967.
(Newcastle City Libraries)

Newcastle Central, 2 January 1979. A class 104 dmu is about the leave for West Monkseaton via Wallsend.
(Alan Young)

who, with Richard Grainger, had redesigned the heart of Newcastle city centre in the 1830s and 40s. Robert Stephenson was also involved with Dobson in designing the massive, curving trainshed. The station took three years to build.

The main station buildings on Neville Street are classical in style. Although they are impressive, a still larger structure was planned. While the buildings were under construction, the design was scaled down as an economy measure. The portico was intended to stretch the length of the building: the present, shorter, portico with huge arches was added about 1862, to the designs of Thomas Prosser. In 1854 the Royal Station Hotel was added seamlessly and sympathetically to the east end of the building.

The trainshed's three 60ft wide semi-elliptical spans are the architectural triumph of Newcastle Central. 'Built on a sharp curve, to fit with the rear wall of the frontage block which was also curved, they created a spectacular vista. The central span was higher than the others, resting on wide-spaced plain tapered columns with shallow-bracketed two-tier cross girders matching the curves of the roof ribs, only every third of which rested directly over a column. The bracing of the two tiers was said to be in the Gothic style, but Dobson covered them with regular panelled boarding to tone with the classical frontage' (Biddle, 1973).

Viewed from the concourse or the platforms, the structure is dramatic. So successful was this first huge arched trainshed that many others followed such as at York, Manchester Central, and London St. Pancras.

Six platforms were increased to nine in 1871, and twelve in 1877. The piecemeal growth of the station resulted in a peculiar system of platform numbering: 1 to 9 followed by A1, A4, A5, B, and C. From 1894 there were fifteen platforms (numbered conventionally) after the addition of three 'suburban' platforms, an associated concourse ('Tynemouth Square') and ticket office at the east end. Two further spans were added to the trainshed at this time. These developments brought the station site up to 39,600 square yd (slightly over 8 acres) in area, 7½ acres roofed, with a total platform length of 3,000yd. Only three platforms dealt with through traffic: East Coast main line expresses called at number 8 (the longest, at 1,100ft), and 9-10 was an island platform reached by a footbridge approached by a ramp from the concourse, also by both a ramp and steps from platform 9.

Train movements were controlled by seven signal cabins. The main one, containing 244 levers, was No.1 at the east end of the station. No.2, with 57 levers, controlled the main through platforms, while No.3 at the west end controlled the approach to King Edward Bridge. No.4 and High Level cabins were at the east end. Two further cabins were at Dean Street and Forth Banks. Signalling was reorganised by 1909 when a 250-lever cabin (No.1) was constructed on a gantry, replacing Nos.1 and 4,

Dean Street and High Level. Electro-pneumatic signal operation was now complete within and around Central station, extending to Manors and Gateshead.

By the turn of the century a large workforce was employed at Central station. The station master had eleven assistants, with 300 further employees including porters and ticket collectors. In addition there were over 200 booking clerks, almost 100 signalmen, 170 guards, and twenty shunters.

As well as the expanding passenger traffic towards the end of the 19th century, Central station was also handling almost a million parcels, over 20,000 bicycles, and numerous other consignments. Heavier goods traffic was handled at Forth Goods depot as well as at Trafalgar depot (until 2 January 1907, when it was replaced by New Bridge Street, east of the former Blyth & Tyne terminus).

On 1 July 1904 the first third-rail 600v electric suburban trains left Newcastle Central on the route to Tynemouth and New Bridge Street. The service was supplemented from 1 January 1909 by electric trains direct to Benton via the new Manors East to New Bridge Street connection. In 1917 the full circular Central-Central service began. The tracks at platforms 1 to 6 were equipped with electrified third rails. The track at platform 7 was later electrified to handle South Shields electric trains as necessary.

Further major changes took place on 1 October 1906 when King Edward Bridge opened. Since 1850 East Coast main line services entered or left Central station via the three-track High Level Bridge, reversing to continue their journey. This lengthened journey times and added operating problems at the busy junction immediately east of the station. The four tracks of King Edward Bridge allowed through running, and the triangular junction at the Gateshead end permitted greater flexibility of operation, so that, if necessary, Sunderland line services could also use the new bridge.

Central station was one of the largest and busiest in Britain. In 1911, 3,054,004 tickets were issued. Apart from express and local stopping services on the East Coast, the Coast Circle and South Shields lines, there were trains to Carlisle, Hawick via Reedsmouth, Middlesbrough via Sunderland or Fencehouses; and more local services to Dunston-on-Tyne, and to Blackhill and Consett via Rowland's Gill or Annfield Plain. On the busiest days some 750 trains were handled. Employment at the station grew, reaching 730 by 1924. Whilst the increasingly fast main line services attracted most attention, an important suburban development was the long-planned introduction of electric trains to South Shields in 1938. For twenty years, starting in the late 1920s, the scene at Newcastle Central was enlivened by the comings and goings of Sentinel Cammell and Clayton steamcars on the Blackhill via Rowland's Gill and the North Wylam services, and, for a short time before its closure on 17 June 1929, the Ponteland / Darras Hall line.

In the British Railways era the variety of services

Class A4 4-6-2 No. 60026 'Miles Beevor' stands in platform 8 at Newcastle Central with 'The Fair Maid' from Kings Cross to Perth on 16 June 1958.   *(N. E. Stead Collection)*

operating out of Newcastle Central declined. As early as May 1926 the LNER had withdrawn the Dunston service at the start of the General Strike and never restored it. The Washington service all but disappeared by 1948, although it struggled on until the 'Beeching axe' fell in 1963. Blackhill's trains from Newcastle via Rowland's Gill were withdrawn on 1 February 1954, to be followed by the Annfield Plain route on 23 May 1955. The Hawick service ceased on 15 October 1956.

The closures just mentioned affected lines with few trains and had little impact on the use of Newcastle Central, which, with almost fifteen million passengers in 1958, was the busiest station outside London. In that year the station received modern electric lighting, whilst in 1957 colour-light signalling was introduced throughout the station. In 1959 a new signal box was commissioned, situated unobtrusively on platforms 8 and 9. This controlled ten miles of track and replaced numbers 1 to 3 and Manors cabins. By the late-1950s the number of trains per day had declined in comparison with the 1920s, ranging from about 520 on winter weekdays to just over 600 on the busiest summer Saturday. The staff had decreased to 569 by 1960. Tickets sales, however, were 11% higher than in 1911.

From the late-1950s to early-1960s there was a more-or-less fixed pattern of train arrivals and departures at Central's platforms. At the east end, 1 to 3 were used by Coast Circle electric trains, whilst the South Shields electrics used platform 6. Trains starting from Newcastle and serving Alnwick, Berwick, and Edinburgh used the longer platform 4, whilst Sunderland line trains departed from platform 5. Platform 7 dealt with the infrequent Tyne Commission Quay trains, also parcels traffic. Platforms 8, 9 and 10 were signalled for bi-directional main line workings. The west end platforms numbered 11, 12 and 13 handled parcels, whilst Hexham and Carlisle trains used platforms 14 and 15. South of the station were four through goods lines.

During the 1960s Newcastle Central saw major changes in motive power on passenger and goods services. The familiar smell of steam engines vanished from the trainshed of the Central station, to be replaced with diesel fumes. Diesel multiple units took over most of the Carlisle duties in 1958-59 and Alnwick by 1961. On main line expresses the much admired A4 streamliners, introduced in 1935, handed over to Deltic diesels (Class 55). Even the familiar electrics yielded to diesel multiple units; first the South Shields trains on 7 January 1963, then the Coast Circle trains on 17 June 1967.

After a lull, withdrawal of passenger train services affecting Newcastle Central resumed in the 1960s, beginning with Washington on 9 September 1963. The closure on 2 November 1964 of the Blyth and Newbiggin branches hardly affected Central station, since almost every train used Manors North as the Newcastle terminus. On 29 January 1968 the 'local' service to Alnwick ceased, but two weekday trains continued operating to Alnmouth, three miles short of Alnwick. On 11 March 1968 the North Wylam route to Hexham closed, all trains being diverted via Blaydon.

The 1970s saw remarkable changes to Central station's suburban services. Following a decline in use of Coast Circle and South Shields trains, the *Tynerider* promotion of 1970 increased their popularity. Bright orange signs directed passengers to the 'Tynerider' ticket office (the east office) and welcomed them to the trains. In 1972-73 the roofing over the suburban platforms (but not 'Tynemouth Square' concourse) was removed; if it was raining, the Tyneriders would now get wet! In 1973 construction of the Metro system was approved, which would divert all South Shields and Coast Circle trains underground through the city centre, with a 'Central' Metro station beneath the existing station. This project required temporary removal of the east end of the portico. Demolition took place in late-1977, but the damage was soon made good. To allow conversion to Metro operation, the Central to West Monkseaton service via Benton was withdrawn on 23 January 1978, and trains to Tynemouth ceased from 11 August 1980. On 1 June 1981 the South Shields service was withdrawn. Since then the only suburban services have been towards Sunderland and Hexham. The latter service was diverted via King Edward Bridge from 4 October 1982. A limited suburban service continued on the East Coast main line northbound serving Manors, Cramlington, and Morpeth, and Chester-le-Street and Durham southbound.

Central Metro Station opened on 15 November 1981. A staircase and lift descend from the main-line station concourse to the ticketing level of the Metro station, which is also reached by pedestrian staircases from Grainger Street and Neville Street. There are further escalators, stairs, and a lift down to the Metro platforms.

With most suburban traffic transferred to the Metro, platforms 1 to 4 were demolished by 1990 to make way for a car park. The opportunity was taken to rationalise the track layout east of the station, so the diamond crossing – which had reputedly been the world's largest – was drastically simplified in 1990. Newcastle Central signal box has been closed and replaced by a new one close to Gateshead shed. A new island platform has been constructed south of the existing platforms to handle through workings between the Sunderland and Carlisle lines. These major alterations have made it necessary to renumber the platforms.

PLATFORM NUMBERING FROM 1991

Old	New	Additional island platform	
1 to 6	out of use	North face	
7	1	5	(east end)
8	2	6	(west end)
9	3	South face	
10	4 (straightened)	7	(east end)
11	9	8	(west end)
12	10		
13	11		
14	12		
15	out of use		

Within the station, in 1985 the ticket and enquiry office was relocated across the concourse inside a see-through shell, on the site of the former newsagent's. The city corporation insisted that its design should contrast with the rest of the station. In common with other major stations, the concourse has been re-laid with off-white Celtic Marble tiles, making the area much brighter. On the platforms outside the trainshed electric lamps of 1970s vintage have given way to 1990s designs. The final major change has been the re-introduction of electric train services to Central station. Electrification between Newcastle and York was mooted by the NER shortly before the grouping of 1923, but the LNER took the idea no further. In 1991 the East Coast main line from London King's Cross to Edinburgh Waverley was electrified at 25,000 volts a/c providing the fastest long-distance service in Britain with trains at half-hourly intervals to and from King's Cross.

During 150 years of remarkable changes in technology, travelling habits and architectural fashions, Newcastle Central has continued to serve its purpose. The fine original buildings and trainshed have survived. The misguided 1960s vision of making Newcastle the 'Brasilia of the North' did not progress down Grainger Street and sweep the station away: thankfully Newcastle Central has not been turned into another London Euston, Birmingham New Street or Leeds City!

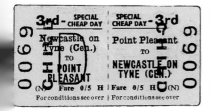

Central Station concourse in August 1998. The Celtic Marble tiled floor gleams beneath the stately curved roof. To the left, the Travel Centre opened in 1985. *(Alan Young)*

A class 101 dmu arrives from West Monkseaton via Wallsend on 30 December 1978. *(Alan Young)*

The suburban section of Newcastle Central in August 1973. Removal of the awnings had been progressing for two years and was still underway on platforms 7 and 8 (left).
(Alan Young)

New and old at Newcastle on 30 August 1979. The 'Inter City 125' on the left with its class 43 loco at each end had recently supplanted the Deltic as prestige motive power on the East Coast Main Line. 55018 'Ballymoss'.
(Alan Young)

High Level Bridge from the Gateshead bank of the Tyne.
(Alan Young)

Coast Circle Stations

No other suburban railway in Britain could match the variety of stations found in British Railways days on the Coast Circle. There were handsome rural stations, long since engulfed by urban growth, such as Benton and South Gosforth. At Backworth there was a truly countrified station. There were unashamedly suburban stations at West Jesmond and Heaton. Elaborate seaside stations were represented by Monkseaton, Whitley Bay, and Tynemouth. In total contrast were the functional LNER additions at West Monkseaton and Longbenton. Most impressive was Newcastle Central, of national importance for its architecture. While most possessed just two side platforms, Heaton station had two islands. The total platform accommodation was eight at Tynemouth, nine at Manors, and fifteen at Newcastle.

The variety of stations in part reflected their ages. 1860s buildings were represented by Jesmond; 1870s by Benton; 1880s by Manors East; and the 1890s by West Jesmond (actually opened in 1900). Manors North represented the first decade of the 20th Century, West Monkseaton the 1930s, and Longbenton the 1940s.

The variety also reflects the role of different companies in constructing the stations. For example the Newcastle & North Shields produced Percy Main; the York, Newcastle & Berwick created Newcastle Central; the Blyth & Tyne gave us South Gosforth; the North Eastern rebuilt Walker Gate; and the LNER added West Monkseaton.

The differing functions of the stations also help to explain their variety. Newcastle Central was a major inter-city station and the hub of the regional and local network. South Gosforth and Benton were built for small communities, but later they coped with massive increases in passengers. South Gosforth also found itself serving as a junction. Monkseaton, Whitley Bay, and Tynemouth were rebuilt between 1882 and 1915 to handle swelling numbers of day-trippers, holidaymakers, and commuters. Monkseaton's enlargement also anticipated traffic on the Collywell Bay branch, which failed to open. Manors grew in stages into a sprawling mass of platforms. It was rebuilt when the main line was widened in 1887, and had five more platforms added for traffic diverted from the former New Bridge Street station. It developed as an interchange point, but also served the east end of Newcastle's business district.

The LNER added 'cosmetic' uniformity to the stations. Wooden nameboards of a design possibly unique to this line were installed at both ends of the platforms. These had a triangular addition above and below the centre of the board and survived until about 1960. When Longbenton was opened in 1947 the LNER had presumably forgotten about their earlier line-style, and a standard wooden board with raised letters was used. The LNER also installed dignified swans-neck lamp standards with little cream nameplates which remained at most stations until 1971. Benton obstinately remained gas-lit until about 1961.

British Railways North Eastern Region added

Manors North, viewed from Trafalgar Street in 1966.

(Newcastle City Libraries)

tangerine direction, platform number and station name signs during the 1950s and early-1960s. Each station received vitreous enamel nameboards at the 'running-in' end of the platform (with a more generous allocation at North Shields) in about 1960. Totem signs appeared first at Benton and West Monkseaton, in the latter case, probably to replace experimental lamp nameplates based on the unusual LNER nameboard design. In the early 1960s totems appeared at Backworth, Percy Main, Howdon-on-Tyne, and Walker Gate. Benton's totems disappeared early, when the gas lamps were replaced by fluorescent lighting with the station name on the diffuser. In 1970-71 stations were re-lit using massive standards, spaced more widely than the old lamps. Most of the station nameplates then disappeared, but only in 1973-74 did the stations receive British Rail 'corporate identity' nameplates on their lamps, and lose their tangerine nameboards. Benton, North Shields, Percy Main, and Heaton were out-of-step with the other stations in these changes, and details are given in the following station-by-station guide.

The conversion of most of the route to Metro operation resulted in all stations, except Central, Manors East, and Tynemouth having periods of closure. Most stations were altered to meet new needs: trains would be shorter, and staff would no longer be at hand to deter trouble-makers in an age when graffiti and mindless destruction were rife. Some stations, such as Longbenton and West Monkseaton, needed little alteration: LNER austerity had come into its own! Some were retained with minor changes because destruction would be resented, such as Monkseaton and Whitley Bay. Stations from Percy Main to Walker Gate were demolished and rebuilt simply. The huge Tynemouth station was to be abandoned, but public pressure caused the Metro planners to reconsider. It was retained and has been splendidly restored. The charming South Gosforth was transformed into the control centre for the Metro, so a big angular structure has replaced the original buildings. As a token gesture, the NER footbridge has been spared.

Around the Coast Circle, additional stations of simple designs have appeared, as at Shiremoor, and a more ambitious new road/rail interchange is located at Four Lane Ends. Off the original Circle are underground stations such as Jesmond, which are smart and functional. Stations carry nameboards and other signs in Metro house-style of Newcastle cadmium yellow with lower case print, and the big 'M' signs outside. The tall lamps favoured by B.R. Eastern Region have been retained, with slightly smaller bulb-boxes. The Metro has therefore removed some of the variety from the Coast Circle stations, but the best of the old has been kept, and there are more stations than ever to visit!

The curved frontage of Manors East on 5 April 1980.

(Alan Young)

Manors

Generally known as 'The' Manors, the name refers to the area of Newcastle which was almost obliterated by the station as it grew into an extravagant nine-platform affair. A journey through the station on the Benton line gave the traveller a vivid impression of the station's vastness. First the Wallsend line platforms (8 and 9) curved off to the right, followed by the main line platforms (6 and 7), and finally the train stopped at platform 1, with numbers 2 (for trains from Benton to Newcastle) and terminal platforms 3, 4 and 5 (for Blyth and Newbiggin trains) to the right. *(The 1960s platform numbering is used throughout this text.)*

The earliest Manors station opened on 1 July 1847 when passenger services began between Newcastle and Tweedmouth. After 1850, when North Shields trains were diverted from Carliol Square into Central, the two miles between Newcastle and Heaton Junction became congested. In 1887 this section was quadrupled, and Manors was rebuilt with four platforms. The entrance was through a three-storey brick building in which passengers climbed to the elevated platforms. It was on a cramped site, its curving frontage following the line of Melbourne Street. The platform buildings were predominantly of timber, and the platforms were sheltered by heavy-looking slate and corrugated iron awnings.

When the B&T terminus was abandoned on 1 January 1909, Manors was extended to accommodate Central to Benton trains. A building was constructed facing Carliol Square providing a main entrance to the new platforms, but it also served the 1887 platforms. This building was in brick and was single-storeyed, containing a booking hall, waiting rooms, toilets and offices. The entrance was surmounted by a giant gable and a cupola-cum-clock turret. Glazed awnings covered the major part of the new platforms. There was access also from New Bridge Street overbridge at the north end of platforms 1 and 2. This little-used facility was abandoned after fire damage in the early 1960s. Within Manors, movement between platforms was by footbridges stretching between numbers 1 and 9, and subways were provided within the old and new sections of the station.

Although in practice one station, and the nameboards bore the name Manors, platforms 1 to 5 were officially Manors North and 6 to 9 Manors East from 1 January 1909 until 20 February 1969. Some tickets referred to East and North, as did some LNER timetables. B.R. timetables indicated by footnotes that express services from Monkseaton via the main line called at the East rather than the North platforms.

On a typical weekday in the early-1960s, outside rush-hours, an electric multiple unit called every twenty minutes to the Coast via Benton (platform 1), and to the Coast via Wallsend (platform 8), from the Coast via Benton (platform 2), and from the Coast via Wallsend (platform 9), totalling twelve services

Manors North looking towards Newcastle Central on 4 July 1973. Platforms 3, 4 and 5 on the left were no longer in passenger use.   *(Alan Young)*

A Metro Cammell unit leaves platform 2 of Manors North for the short journey to Newcastle on 8 January 1978.
(Alan Young)

per hour. In the rush-hour Coast Circle services were frequent but at irregular intervals, and sparse services to and from the Riverside Branch and Blyth/Newbiggin used the station too. A feature of Saturday services was that hourly Blyth/Newbiggin services operated through to Manors, terminating in bay platforms 3, 4 or 5. By the early-1960s these were dmus, though the first working of the day, originating at Newcastle Central, travelling to Newbiggin, and returning to Manors, was steam-hauled to convey mail and parcels. Platforms 6 and 7 had irregular express emu workings to and from the Coast via Benton SE Curve, as well as dmus to Alnwick. Some steam-hauled semi-fast services to Berwick and Edinburgh called at Manors but main line expresses did not stop here. About half of the Alnwick and semi-fast main line services called at Manors. A variety of goods traffic also passed through on all lines, and electric Quayside Branch goods trains terminated here. Long after electric traction on the Quayside Branch had been abandoned in 1964, poles to support the electric wires remained on Manors East platforms.

The variety of passenger services at Manors began to decline on 2 November 1964 when Blyth/Newbiggin trains were withdrawn, making platforms 3, 4 and 5 redundant. Riverside Branch trains ceased from 23 July 1973, but much more significantly all trains were withdrawn from Manors North when the Coast service via Benton ended on

23 January 1978 in preparation for Metro works. The Coast via Wallsend trains continued until 11 August 1980. From that date, only some thirty trains a day, all 'local' services on the main line, called at Manors. This service has deteriorated, and in winter 1998-99 Manors had only six trains stopping on weekdays, five on Saturdays, and none on Sundays. There are, of course, frequent Metro trains to the Coast via Wallsend from the underground station.

In the 1950s and 1960s Manors was busy and well cared for. The North platforms had a light and airy atmosphere, thanks to the glazed roofing. Hanging baskets were a delightful feature in the summer months. The North Eastern Region's 'oriental blue' paint was liberally applied to iron columns and woodwork, though this jarred somewhat with the tangerine signs! LNER electric mint imperial lamps hanging from the awnings in North station, or on hooped standards on the open platforms, lit the station. Small LNER name tablets accompanied the lamps. Under the East platform awnings the electric lighting had LNER brick-shaped diffusers carrying the station name. Tall lamps arrived in 1971 and 'corporate identity' black and white name signs were installed in 1973.

The decline in passenger services from Manors was accompanied by downsizing of the station. By late-1979 the tracks had been lifted from North station, and demolition of the buildings had begun. By Easter 1980 the only buildings remaining were, ironically, on platforms 1 and 9, the 'local' platforms. Northbound main line passengers could use a crude breeze-block shelter, whilst southbound passengers (if there were any) and coast-bound passengers who shared platforms 7 and 8 had to shelter in the subway!

By September 1985 the once-dignified entrance building on platform 1 was being demolished. The clock turret stood proudly above the crumbling remains of the booking hall, but with the clock removed. A tangerine 'British Railways Manors' sign was still fixed to the gable below the turret, together with a recent British Rail sign, reassuring doubters that trains still called. Access to the station was by a lengthy footbridge across the Central Motorway East. On reaching the station there was first a walk through the roofless booking hall, avoiding chunks of fallen masonry, followed by a stretch of some yards along the rubble-strewn platform 1, overhung by awning supports awaiting demolition. Beyond this a causeway crossed the old trackbed to platform 2. To catch a train to Newcastle Central a footbridge then had to be crossed. By 1985 platforms 2 to 5 had gone, and much of their site had been landscaped. The buildings and awnings on platform 9 were removed in 1986.

By 1991 Manors possessed one shortened island platform, with overhead wires installed for the new East Coast main line electrification. The Technopole Business Park on the site of Manors North and in the space between North and East might have been expected to justify an improved service; but, as was said earlier, only three weekday trains each way call here.

Manors (Metro)

The station is entered at ground level, and there are stairs, escalators, and lifts to the two platforms. Although one of the least used stations on the Metro system, Manors stimulated the development of an adjacent multi-screen cinema and the Technopole Business Park.

Demolition underway at Manors North on 29 December 1979. (Alan Young)

In July 1991 the Technopole Business Park is taking shape on the site of Manors North Station. (Alan Young)

38

New Bridge Street

The Blyth & Tyne Railway reached Newcastle in 1864 with a terminus on the edge of the city centre, some 300yd north of the Newcastle & Berwick's Manors station, and 200yd north of the N& B Trafalgar Goods depot. New Bridge Street, like Central, had a building designed by John Dobson. Known as Picton House (and approached from Picton Place), New Bridge Street's building was a modest, but stylish, Italianate structure in ashlar, with a hipped roof. An 1871 B&T timetable called it simply Newcastle (New Bridge).

The Ordnance Survey 25" map of 1894 shows that the station possessed one island platform, as well as a side platform adjacent to the main building. There were several sidings to the east as well as to the north, where there was a two-road engine shed.

New Bridge Street opened on 27 June 1864 and was served by Tynemouth and Morpeth trains. In 1871 weekday departures amounted to only eight trains to Tynemouth and four to Morpeth, increasing to twelve to Tynemouth six years later. For the last few years of its life, New Bridge Street's passenger service was transformed. From 29 March 1904 electric trains ran every fifteen minutes to Benton, with half continuing around the Coast Circle to Newcastle Central.

On 1 January 1909 New Bridge Street closed to passengers, and trains were diverted to Manors North. The four tracks of the newly completed Coast Circle cut down through the New Bridge Street site and also through the large Trafalgar Goods depot. Manors North was constructed partly on the Trafalgar Goods site. Despite being bisected by the new Coast Circle line, New Bridge Street was retained as a goods station. It expanded to the west, involving the demolition of most of Picton Place (but not Picton House), and to the east. A massive reinforced concrete goods warehouse, designed by William Bell (NER Chief Architect from 1877 to 1914) was constructed in the eastern part of the goods station and completed in 1912. It was not attractive, but it was a prominent feature of the townscape, and remarkably futuristic and functional when compared with some of Bell's other designs, such as Manors North of 1909 and Whitley Bay (1910). The warehouse was badly damaged by an air raid in September 1941 and burned fiercely for some weeks. The most severely damaged sections were demolished, and the building continued to serve as a goods depot, concentrating on fruit and vegetable traffic.

Goods services were withdrawn from New Bridge Street on 4 December 1967, but many years elapsed before the site was cleared. The decaying concrete hulk of the warehouse survived, remarkably, into the 1980s. Central Motorway East, part of the ambitious 1960s plans for the 'motorisation' of central Newcastle, cuts into the western edge of the station site.

New Bridge Street Goods Depot on 4 January 1973, after closure. The huge concrete structure was built in 1912 but severely damaged by fire in 1941.

(Alan Young)

Jesmond

Jesmond was one of the original stations on the B&T New Bridge Street to Monkseaton line, opened on 27 June 1864. It was then on the outskirts of the built-up area. The station's rural character survived until the 1960s, and this possibly encouraged the staff to maintain it and to cultivate the station garden. Their efforts were rewarded by certificates won in the NE Region's Best Kept Stations competition, displayed in the booking hall.

The buildings towards the north end of the down platform consisted of a Gothic booking hall built of brick with stone quoins, with a separate stationmaster's house, which survived until the 1970s. This was of similar materials and was decorated with massive bargeboards. On the up platform was a wooden shelter reminiscent of a large rabbit hutch.

Inner suburban stations proved vulnerable to competition from road transport, and Jesmond booked the least passengers of any Coast Circle station apart from Backworth. The light use resulted in withdrawal of winter Sunday services between 1964 and 1970. Total closure came on 23 January 1978. A single track for empty Metro stock movements is retained through the old station.

In 1998 the platforms were intact, and the waiting shelter and station building remained: the latter was used as *The Carriage* public house. On the same platform, a new structure in the style of a signal box and an old railway coach were the premises of *Valley Junction* Indian Restaurant.

Jesmond (Metro)

This underground station, opened with the line on 11 August 1980, is of deck concourse design with lift and stair access to the platforms.

West Jesmond

Towards the end of the 19th Century, housing spread around the railway between Jesmond and South Gosforth. The NER opened West Jesmond on 1 December 1900 to serve this newly urbanised area. Its single-storey station buildings were in the fashionable Domestic Revival style. Red brick was used in their construction, also for the wall along the rear of the platforms, instead of the customary fence. The main building on the up platform had a half-timbered gable on its frontage, whilst the down platform building was simpler. Glass awnings with glazed end screens protected the platforms for the length of the buildings. A subway connected the platforms. The signal box stood a few yards south of the down platform.

The down and up platform awnings were removed by 1972 and 1977 respectively. Whilst lighting and signing were modernised in the early 1970s, an LNER name sign survived at the up platform entrance until 1977. West Jesmond closed from 23 January 1978 until 11 August 1980 for Metro conversion. The buildings have been retained but the platforms have been shortened. A footbridge has also been built.

By the standards of the Circle stations West Jesmond's passenger bookings were light. With Jesmond it closed on winter Sundays from 1964 until 1970. Goods traffic was handled in sidings at the south end of the up platform until 14 August 1967.

Moor Edge

According to B&T records a station or halt existed, near to the present Ilford Road Metro station, to deal with Town Moor race traffic.

Ilford Road

This standard Metro station was opened on 11 August 1980. It is unusual in having neither a footbridge nor a subway. Ticketing facilities are provided on both platforms, so passengers have no need to cross the line.

Since closure in 1978, the main building at Jesmond has been converted into a pub and restaurant. It is supplemented by an ex GNR carriage.
(Alan Young)

Jesmond looking north some time after 1909 when the terminus for inbound trains was changed from New Bridge Street to Manors North. *(Newcastle City Libraries)*

A Manors to Benton service calls at West Jesmond about 1910. The glazed awnings were removed in the 1970s. *(Newcastle City Libraries)*

South Gosforth

Its situation in a grassy cutting, its gardens, and its Victorian buildings gave South Gosforth a rural atmosphere. The station was one of the original group opened in 1864. Known at first as Gosforth, 'South' was added on 1 March 1905 when West Gosforth opened on the Ponteland Branch. A loop line was installed on the up side south of the station, where the Ponteland autocar could stand between services. A water column also stood here, surviving into the 1960s. The signal box stood behind the southern end of the up platform, with an overhang because of the constricted site.

The layout of buildings at South Gosforth was like that at Jesmond. The stationmaster's house and booking hall were on the down platform, supplemented by quaint wooden sheds. On the up side was a brick waiting room. Like Jesmond and West Jesmond, South Gosforth was one of the quieter stations on the Coast Circle.

On 23 January 1978 South Gosforth closed for Metro construction work. Some months earlier, all up platform buildings had been demolished to make way for the Metro Control Centre. When it re-opened on 11 August 1980 the station was unrecognisable. Even the up platform waiting room had disappeared, and a modern shelter was in its place. As a concession to the past, the NER iron footbridge was retained.

South Gosforth station handled goods traffic until 14 August 1967.

Longbenton

On 14 July 1947 the LNER opened Longbenton to serve the Ministry of Pensions and National Insurance offices which had relocated from London. The station was locally known as 'Ministry Halt', and until the 1960s was recorded as Longbenton Halt in Railway Clearing House documents. From the opening there was a restricted weekday-only service, but the development of Longbenton estate promised plentiful off-peak traffic too, so a full weekday service started in winter 1954-55, and by 1958 almost all trains called on Sundays as well.

The station was built in red brick. Its main features were a pilastered entrance to the up platform building (the side of the line where the 'Ministry' was situated) containing the booking hall, and simple awnings on both platforms. A covered footbridge, also in brick, connected the platforms. Standard LNER mint imperial swans-neck electric lamps with cream and black name tablets, and wooden nameboards with relief lettering were installed. Access was provided by 1956 from the new estate to the down platform, and waiting rooms were soon added on each platform. These were partly dismantled in the early 1970s following damage by vandals, who also kept the station daubed with graffiti.

The station closed on 23 January 1978 for Metro work, re-opening on 11 August 1980 with few changes. The buildings, awnings, and footbridge were retained and cleaned, but the platforms shortened. An additional footbridge with ramp access was built at the east end. To complement the major improvements being made on the adjacent estate, the station was largely rebuilt in 1999.

Long Benton

Four Lane Ends Metro station has obliterated all traces of Long Benton, one of the original stations of 1864. It had a short life, closing on 1 January 1871, to be replaced by Benton. One of its buildings, a simple brick structure with a pitched roof, survived into the era of electrification. By the 1960s a level area beside the line and an NER style platform fence to the north of the line were all that remained.

Four Lane Ends

This deck concourse road/rail interchange station opened on the first day of Metro services. From its opening some bus routes were altered to serve the station, and about 150 car parking spaces were provided. Facilities include lift and escalator access to the platforms, a travel centre, Metro police office, and a newsagent's kiosk.

A class 104 unit draws into South Gosforth on 24 July 1977. Construction of the Metro Control Centre is proceeding alongside the down platform. *(Alan Young)*

In 1973, the tangerine running in boards were replaced by small 'corporate identity' signs. These, in turn, soon gave way to similar ones with the correct spelling.
(Alan Young)

Longbenton, 8 January 1978. The station is adorned with folk art courtesy of Benton Agro Boys, Longbenton Killer Squad and other well wishers.
(Alan Young)

11 August 1980, the first day of Metro service, a train for Haymarket enters Longbenton.
(Alan Young)

Benton

When the B&T Newcastle line opened in 1864 no station was provided here, although there was a Benton station (renamed Forest Hall on 1 December 1874) on the East Coast main line. The present Benton station opened on 1 March 1871, replacing Long Benton and Forest Hall. Benton was similar in character to Jesmond and South Gosforth, although built seven years later.

The brick-built station house on the up platform was combined with offices, toilets, and waiting room. The gable of the two-storey station house faced the platform, and the house extended to meet the lofty single-storey booking hall. This presented a bay window and a gable to the platform, almost as tall as the station house. A veranda, supported by columns, stretched between the gables, and was enclosed to create a waiting room. A porters' office was also in this section. Further office space, including the booking hall, was in a single-storey wooden extension under a tall slated pitched roof east of the main building. A single-storey flat-roofed extension at the opposite end housed a public lavatory. Beside this extension was a small wooden shed.

On the down platform was an attractive brick shelter with a tall slate hipped roof topped by iron cresting and finials. An iron NER footbridge connected the platforms. A few yards north east of the down platform was the tall Benton signal box, built with double overhangs because of the constricted site.

Happily the station remains almost intact on the Metro. However, the wooden booking office has been replaced by a covered ticketing area, and the NER footbridge has been superseded by a modern structure.

Platform lighting has differed from the standardised pattern on the Coast Circle. In Edwardian times the platforms were lit by gas lanterns on small standards, but they gave way to tall, elaborate posts of a design seldom seen in stations, with 'Sugg' style gas lamps hanging from them. These survived until about 1961, long after electric lighting was installed at the other Circle and Riverside stations. N.E. Region totems were fixed to the standards. The gas lamps and totems were replaced by fluorescent strip lamps with 'Benton' printed on the diffusers. By 1977 the strip lighting had been replaced with smaller lamps. Eventually Benton stepped into line when the Metro's tall vandal-proof lamps were installed. British Rail 'corporate identity' nameplates were not installed at Benton.

The goods sidings west of the up platform were abandoned on 14 August 1967. However, when the station temporarily closed on 23 January 1978 the former sidings were revived as a Metro construction base.

Despite its limited importance as a generator of traffic, Benton has enjoyed the role of a terminus. From 1909 until 1917 the New Bridge Street electric service terminated here, and some Metro trains from Pelaw end their journey at Benton. Part of the former North West curve to the East Coast main line now serves as two sidings for these terminating trains.

Forest Hall

Opened in 1864, this station stood about half-a-mile north-east of the present Benton station. It closed on 1 January 1871 when Benton was opened. As late as the 1960s a short section of platform wall could still be seen close to Benton East Junction.

Benton looking towards the Coast in 1959.   (Stations UK)

Palmersville

This Metro station opened on 19 March 1986 immediately south-west of Great Lime Road bridge. Each of the two platforms is approached by a covered stairway and an open ramp, and metal shelters with curved roofs are provided.

Benton Square

This was a latecomer, opened on 1 July 1909 to serve Benton Square Colliery and its cottages. Its site was immediately to the north-east of Great Lime Road bridge. Its two long, wooden platforms were devoid of buildings, and the small roadside booking office was above station level where a path led to the up platform. It closed on 20 September 1915. By the 1960s the station had completely disappeared.

Backworth

When opened in 1864 this station was called Hotspur, but it was renamed Backworth in June 1865. It replaced Backworth (originally called Holywell) on the B&T Percy Main branch.

Backworth's two platforms were on a curve of 17 chains radius. Until the early 1970s a bridge carrying Backworth Waggonway crossed the station halfway along the platforms. The original station building was on the up platform. It was a single-storey brick structure with closely set twin pavilions, each with stone bay windows projecting onto the platform, and topped with stone finials. A short awning linked the pavilions. On the down side a brick shelter with a glazed front and roof sloping away from the tracks was replaced in the mid-1960s with a metal-and-glass 'bus shelter'. Apparently, owing to an oversight, this new shelter had no entrance when it was constructed!

From at least 1904 the booking office was in a functional wooden shed on the overbridge at the east end of the station.

Blyth/Newbiggin branch trains to and from Manors North called at Backworth until 2 November 1964, allowing passengers from stations between Jesmond and Benton to change here.

From the 1950s Backworth was the least used station on the Circle and the opportunity was taken to replace it with a Metro station half a mile east at Shiremoor. Closure came on 13 June 1977, and demolition began within six weeks.

Shiremoor

This Metro station, of standard design with two slightly staggered platforms, opened on 11 August 1980. Nexus launched an unusual experiment here. In early 1998 the music of Delius was broadcast over loudspeakers to drive away vandals who had been causing a nuisance. Apparently vandals don't like Delius!

The short lived Benton Square Station looking towards Newcastle. The booking office is the wooden building to the left of the bridge.   *(Newcastle City Libraries)*

This page top: Backworth station 27 July 1976.
(Alan Young)

Middle: The booking hall viewed from the roadbridge.
(Alan Young)

Bottom: By 24 July 1977, Backworth was closed and the wooden booking hall removed. The view is towards the Coast. *(Alan Young)*

CENTRE PAGE PHOTOGRAPHS

Left Upper: Platforms 1 and 2 at Manors on 29 March 1972. The train of Metro Cammell stock has come from Newcastle via the Riverside branch and the Coast and will soon be back at its starting point. *(Alan Young)*

Left Lower: Waiting for the coast train at South Gosforth on 14 August 1973. The Metro control centre stands on the site of this building.
(Alan Young)

Right Upper: New station name. New train livery. 4059 brings up the rear of a St James to the Coast service at Meadow Well (formerly Smith's Park) on 15 August 1998. *(Alan Young)*

Right Lower: If the Metro reaches Sunderland, it will restore passenger service to Monkwearmouth. The new station will be just to the south of the original 1848 structure which closed in 1967 and is now a museum. The magnificent but grimy facade is seen in April 1954 being passed by an earlier generation of electric traction. Sunderland tram No.96 was built in 1933. It remained in service until this, the last route from Seaburn to Fawcett Street in the town centre, closed on 1 October 1954.
(Colour Rail)

The flat roofed concrete booking hall at West Monkseaton was built in 1933. Photographed in 1976, it has been retained as the Metro Station entrance. *(Alan Young)*

West Monkseaton

The LNER opened this station in the 2½ mile gap between Backworth and Monkseaton to serve new housing developments. Unlike the other Circle stations, the platforms were wooden. Building was swift: the plans and estimates were approved on 17 February 1933 and it was opened on 20 March 1933 by the Chairman of Whitley Bay and Monkseaton Urban District Council. The booking hall on the overbridge demonstrated the 1930s 'utilitarian clean-line' styling. It was of concrete, with a flat roof, and included a kiosk either side of the entrance. LNER 'fish' logos were displayed above the entrance.

Originally there were small wooden waiting rooms on each platform and a ticket booth at the western end of the up platform. Swans-neck electric lamp standards were installed. Minor features of interest were nameboards and lamp nameplates with triangular additions above and below. The nameboards also had three lamps to illuminate them. A slanted concrete awning was later added to the up platform, fronting the waiting room and extending to the steps to the entrance block.

West Monkseaton benefited from B.R. rush-hour express services, calling at Manors then stations from West Monkseaton to North Shields. The off-peak express service of 1967-70 also called here.

The direct Newcastle line closed on 23 January 1978 for Metro works, and until 10 September 1979 the service via Wallsend terminated at West Monkseaton. A period of closure ended on 11 August 1980 when the Metro was opened.

In 1998 the LNER entrance building was still standing, but shorter, concrete platforms had been built. The old concrete supports for the up platform awning remained in use.

Monkseaton (First station)

The original Monkseaton station opened on 31 October 1860 on the Hartley to Tynemouth line, and lasted until 25 July 1915 when the present station replaced it on a new alignment. It was known as Whitley until 3 July 1882.

The original station was smaller than its replacement, with two paved platforms. On the up side the main building was in brick, with round-headed windows. The hipped roof was topped by iron cresting and paired chimney stacks. From the building a hipped awning sheltered the platform. The end walls extended to create screens, pierced by paired, round-headed windows. On the other platform stood a smaller building and the signal box. A level crossing was at the north end of the station, and the Avenue Branch and New Bridge Street line parted company immediately to its north.

Nothing remains of this station.

Monkseaton (Second station)

Passenger bookings at Monkseaton rose spectacularly from 80,219 in 1901 to 241,313 in 1911, after electrification. This increase, together with plans for a new electrified route to Collywell Bay and track remodelling, justified the building of the present station which opened on 25 July 1915.

The Chief Architect of the NER, William Bell, designed the new stations at Monkseaton and Whitley Bay. At Monkseaton, three-platform faces were provided. The down platform, with the main buildings, was a side platform. The up platform was an island with an electrified terminating line at its other face. A wonderful array of iron columns supported a huge curved glazed roof over the down platform, creating a wide, well-lit space under cover. Glazed end-screens and an extended awning towards the track provided additional comfort for passengers. All of the architect's imagination went into the glasswork: the brick buildings with a hipped, slate roof were dull, and the frontage had only two large gables breaking the roof-line to add a little interest. On the up platform a large, ridged glazed awning covered the undistinguished buildings. Other features of Monkseaton station were the covered ramps from the Marine Drive overbridge to the platforms, and the wide gap between the running lines that, until at least 1967, enclosed well-tended lawns.

The awning over the island platform was removed in about 1971. The buildings, never intended to be seen without the awning, looked lost on the bleak expanse of platform.

For much of its life Monkseaton was both junction and terminating station for the Blyth/Newbiggin trains via the Avenue Branch. The promised electric service to Collywell Bay, which would have used the first mile of the Avenue Branch, never materialised.

Signal boxes were Monkseaton West, in the angle between the Avenue Branch and the Coast Circle, and East, on the up side of the line. The latter controlled electrified sidings that had small bays into the east end of the up platform. It also supervised sidings on the site of the 'inland' Blyth & Tyne route of 1864 and the terminating line behind the island platform. These sidings survived into the 1960s after goods closure took place on 2 March 1959.

In late B.R. days Monkseaton remained a major station, handling commuter and day-trip traffic. It closed for Metro works on 10 September 1979 and re-opened on 11 August 1980 with its main buildings and glazed covering over the up platform retained and redecorated.

By 1998 the down platform covered ramp and the extended awning had been removed, but stained glass had been installed in the east end-screen, depicting local scenes. The up platform retained its covered ramp, and had small, modern shelters.

Monkseaton looking towards Whitley Bay in 1959. The splitting signal controls the junction for Blyth and Newbiggin.
(Stations UK)

Whitley Bay (First station)

Opened on 3 July 1882 as Whitley (renamed Whitley Bay on 1 July 1899) this station had ridge-and-furrow awnings over both platforms. These awnings had vertical, rather than the hipped, ends found at the 1882 station at Tynemouth. The covered footbridge was of the type that survives at Cullercoats. It was replaced by the larger, second station.

Whitley Bay (Second station)

Within a mile of Monkseaton is another fine, large station at Whitley Bay. The present structure opened on 9 October 1910, replacing that of 1882. The forecourt of the new station marks the site of its predecessor.

The new station was built to handle the increased passenger traffic that developed after the 1904 electrification. Commuters were settling in the town, and many day-trippers made the journey to the coast from Newcastle at weekends in summer. Whitley Bay was thriving as a holiday resort and was especially popular with Glaswegians. It is still one of the busiest Tyneside stations.

Whitley Bay station was designed by William Bell. A massive red brick clock tower greeted the passengers who approached via the Esplanade and Station Road. The tower enclosed a small portico and was decorated with lighter brick string-courses, terra cotta fruit, and an ogee-shaped top. Two further porticoes flanked the clock tower. Until the mid-1970s small, glazed awnings stretched between them and the clock tower.

Inside the station, the two platforms were covered by a glazed trainshed, but the section above the tracks was uncovered. The trainshed construction was in effect two huge, double pitched awnings, spanning the tracks on girders pierced by circular holes, with decorated brackets and good cast-iron work. Lines of pillars in front of the buildings, and towards the platform edges, supported the iron and glass. Two latticework footbridges connected the platforms.

Until the late 1960s the north end of the station was kept immaculate, presumably because most holidaymakers arrived from this direction. On the down platform, the tangerine station name rose out of a floral display. The other end of the station, which also had the signal box on the Tynemouth-bound platform, was not so well groomed.

The conversion of Whitley Bay for the Metro was sensitive and involved relatively little demolition. The major alteration was the shortening of the trainshed, but most of it remains intact. The entrance hall has been decorated with a mosaic of a beach scene.

Cullercoats (First station)

The first Cullercoats station was on the original Hartley to Tynemouth 'inland' route. It opened to passengers on 27 June 1864, closed entirely on 7 July 1882, and was subsequently demolished.

A grubby V2 2-6-2 No.60910 arrives at Whitley Bay with a Summer Saturday train from Glasgow via Newcastle and Wallsend in August 1962.   *(Ian S. Carr)*

Cullercoats (Second station)

Compared with the other three coastal stations, this is a modest structure. It opened on 7 July 1882 on the new coastal alignment of the Hartley-Tynemouth route.

The exterior was similar to Tynemouth, but resembled South Shields even more closely. It was a long, single-storey red brick building with a slate roof. The central section, through which passengers entered, projected forward slightly under a hipped roof, and the building ended with pavilions.

The cramped character of this station was due to the relatively narrow platforms, and to the placing of the buildings at the extreme north end. The signal box formerly stood at the north end of the up (Tynemouth-bound) platform. The awnings were originally of a vertically-ended ridge-and-furrow design, as at the first Whitley Bay station, but by 1926 glazed awnings of a simple longitudinal ridged design had replaced them. The highlight was a covered stepped footbridge south of the buildings, similar to the better known one at Beverley. The platforms were backed by a wall rather than the customary fence.

In Autumn 1900 Cullercoats station was flooded to above platform level. A train was derailed when entering the flood waters, and the stranded passengers were rescued by boats from the nearby beach. Boat owners took advantage of the unfortunate passengers charging a fee for their journey to safety! Further flooding occurred in 1905.

Goods services were withdrawn on 10 February 1964. Passenger trains ceased on 10 September 1979 for Metro works. When re-opened on 11 August 1980, the platforms and awnings were shorter but few other changes had been made. It is now an attractive, well-preserved Victorian station.

Whitley Bay has survived into the Metro era substantially unaltered. 4014 is heading for Heworth via Benton and Newcastle. *(Martin Bairstow)*

Cullercoats looking north in 1973. The covered footbridge is an original 1882 feature but the awnings are more recent. The Metro has brought little change. *(Alan Young)*

The Newcastle & Berwick terminus at Tynemouth is seen in residential use in 1988, over 100 years after closure to passengers, and some 30 after the end of goods traffic. *(Alan Young)*

Tynemouth
(First Blyth & Tyne Railway station)
The southern terminus of the 'inland' route from Hartley opened on 1 April 1861. It was renamed North Shields, later North Shields Terminus from 1865 after a branch was opened to its east on 27 June 1864, the day when through services from New Bridge Street began. At first a temporary structure was provided, but after a few months brick buildings with stone facings were constructed, containing a booking office, a general waiting room, and a first class ladies' room.

This station closed to passengers when the present Tynemouth station came into use on 7 July 1882, but it survived as a goods station, approached from the south. Coal traffic was handled until complete closure on 1 May 1971. The B&T buildings were demolished shortly afterwards.

Tynemouth (Second Blyth & Tyne station)
Because the first station was too far from the beach, this one opened closer to the coast on 27 June 1864, on a branch to the east off the original route from Hartley. It was renamed North Shields Station (as opposed to 'Terminus') in 1865 when the line was extended to a new Tynemouth terminus, closer still to the sea. This station, like North Shields Terminus, was replaced by the present Tynemouth on 7 July 1882, and removed without trace.

Tynemouth (Third Blyth & Tyne station)
In 1865 this new Tynemouth terminus was opened, as noted above. This in turn closed on 7 July 1882 to be replaced by the present Tynemouth station. It no longer survives.

Tynemouth (Newcastle & Berwick station)
The Shields (North Shields) line via Wallsend was extended to this terminus on 29 March 1847. It was opened in the same year and by the same company as the East Coast main line, and its stone, Tudor building was strikingly similar to the stations designed by Benjamin Green, such as Killingworth and Acklington. The two-storey building had a projecting gabled centrepiece with a mullioned oriel window over a three-bay portico with shallow pointed arches and shield motifs. On either side were gabled dormers, and to one end was a single-storey wing with a wooden ventilator. This station incorporated the Royal Hotel.

Although closed to passengers on 3 July 1882, goods traffic was handled until 2 March 1959. The building survives in residential use with Grade II listed status.

Tynemouth (Present station)
This station opened on 7 July 1882, on the new route for through traffic. Designed by William Bell, it was internally elegant and spacious. Its eight platforms and four through tracks gave it the appearance of a major city station. In addition to the two main platforms the up side had three bays at the north end, and four at the south end (one being treated as a siding). The exterior, on Station Terrace, was a long, red brick single-storey structure like that at Cullercoats, but on a larger scale, having a higher

The exterior of Tynemouth Station on 30 December 1978 since when a glazed awning has been installed above the entrance. *(Alan Young)*

Dwarfed by the scale of the station, a Metro Cammell class 101 pauses at Tynemouth on 20 August 1976 before continuing its journey to North Shields and Newcastle. *(Alan Young)*

roof with iron cresting, two chimney stacks on the central section, taller pavilion gables, and rounded windows.

Inside, the wide concourse and platforms were under huge expanses of glass, with a series of double-pitched awnings presenting hipped ends to the platforms, and they were enclosed by glazed end-screens.

A forest of narrow cast-iron columns supported latticework girders along with intricate brackets and spandrels. The curve of the platforms created a spectacular perspective effect. The wide concourse was separated from the up platform by elegant iron railings. For the crowds of visitors, a very wide, covered footbridge was provided, approached by two staircases.

The attractiveness of the station interior was noted both by travellers and officialdom. Joyce (1985) refers to a visitor around 1900 commenting that Tynemouth was 'without a doubt the prettiest station of any large town in this country [with] its charming beds of flowers, its hanging pendants of floral beauty covering its roof and hanging all over its supporting pillars'. Another visitor remarked that it looked more like a garden than a railway station. Between 1900 and 1910 the staff received first, second, and special prizes in the NER Best Kept Station competition. The tradition continued into LNER and British Railways days. A photograph in the *News Guardian* showed the garden in 1956 when yet another first prize had been won.

The scale of the 1882 structure reflected Tynemouth's role as a growing commuter town and as a day-trip and residential holiday resort. Until the 1950s the profusion of platforms handled excursions and summer special workings. However, by the early 1970s Tynemouth station seemed absurdly large with only two platforms in passenger use. There was more the sense of visiting a museum than a functioning railway station. The tiled wall map of the North Eastern Railway, dating from about 1902, remained with various other obsolete features including a warning to 'Beware of the Hoist'.

The case for retaining the station as a Metro stop seemed very weak, and it was proposed that a new 'halt' should be built at the north end of the existing buildings, allowing the station to be demolished. However local residents loved their station, and they obtained the support of the Fine Arts Commission and North Tyneside Council in opposing demolition. Their case was strengthened in 1978 when the buildings were listed Grade II. The newly-formed Friends of Tynemouth Station helped to devise regeneration plans, resulting in the restoration of large sections of canopy in 1988-89. The up platform was widened and straightened, and platform entrances were relocated between the footbridge steps. Imitation gas lamps were installed on each platform. A glazed awning was added to the frontage to good effect. Other uses for the station have been introduced: there are workshop units on the down platform, and on Saturdays both platforms host a fleamarket, drawing crowds to the station, reminiscent of past times.

No. 406

SPECIAL
HALF-DAY
EXCURSION

TO

Darlington
Durham, Newcastle
Tynemouth
AND
Whitley Bay

Sunday, 10th October

	Return Fares, Third Class.			
	To Darlington	To Durham	To Newcastle	To Tynemouth & Whitley Bay
	a.m.			
Leeds (New Station) dep.	11 30			5/6
	p.m.	5/-		
York .... ,,	12 15			
Darlington .... ,,	1 10	—	— 4/11	5/-

The train will return the same day as follows :—

Whitley Bay	....	.... dep.	7 35 p.m.
Tynemouth	....	.... ,,	7 45 ,,
Newcastle	....	.... ,,	8 10 ,,
Durham	....	.... ,,	8 35 ,,
Darlington	....	.... ,,	9 10 ,,

TICKETS CAN BE OBTAINED IN ADVANCE

NO LUGGAGE ALLOWED. CHILDREN over 3 and under 12 years, half-fares. TICKETS are not transferable and are only available to and from stations for which issued and by excursion trains in both directions : they are not available for intermediate stations and must be obtained before travelling or full ordinary fare will be charged. The Tickets are issued subject to General Conditions and Regulations specified in the Company's current time tables. Tickets, bills and all particulars can be obtained at the Stations, or as under :—From Leeds—L.N.E.R. Office, 141, Briggate ; Messrs. Thos. Cook & Son, Ltd., 35, Boar Lane ; Messrs. Dean & Dawson, Ltd., 81, Boar Lane ; Mr. C. A. Hood, opposite Town Hall ; Mr. A. B. Robinson, 81, Woodhouse Lane ; Messrs. Dean & Dawson, Ltd., 7, St. Peter's Street, Huddersfield. From York—Messrs. Thos. Cook & Son, Ltd., 38, Coney Street. For further information apply to the District Passenger Manager, York (Tel. No. 2264).

YORK, October, 1926. 30472—Ben Johnson & Co., Ltd., Printers, York—3,500

Tangerine signs at the entrance to North Shields Tunnel. Note the small print: 'It is dangerous to touch the elevated rail.' *(Alan Young)*

Since 11 August 1980, therefore, thanks to the triumph of sentiment over economics, we have been able to enjoy the incongruous sight of Metro trains at the long platforms under antique awnings.

North Shields
(Newcastle & North Shields Railway)

The first Shields station (renamed North Shields in November 1874) opened as the terminus of the route from Newcastle on 20 June 1839. This had a timber triple arch roof and two platforms, each ending at a turntable. A carriage shed, goods shed and sidings were also provided. The line was extended to a new Tynemouth terminus on 29 March 1847. The timetable for May 1849 showed a service of 23 trains per day each way on Mondays to Fridays, 26 on Saturdays, and 21 on Sundays. It was replaced by the present station in 1890.

North Shields (Present station)

This opened in 1890, replacing the old N&NS station. It was built where the 1882 route from Whitley Bay and Tynemouth emerged from Tynemouth (later North Shields) Tunnel. Access was from a roadside building above the tunnel entrance, and the two platforms were beneath an arched trainshed with a ventilator along its summit, and glazed screens at the western end. Although the ventilator and glazing admitted some daylight, the station was gloomy, made all the more so by the tunnel at the eastern end, and the cutting at the other end. Single-bulb LNER mint imperial lights did little to relieve the gloom.

The station was greatly altered, starting in the late 1950s. By 1959 new N.E. Region tangerine vitreous enamel nameboards had been installed, unusually, at each end of both platforms. In the mid-1960s the trainshed was demolished and replaced by awnings. LNER lighting and nameplates gave way to simple electric lamp standards, with tiny BR 'corporate identity' nameplates fixed to them. The only large 'corporate identity' nameboards found on the Coast Circle were also fitted, in the normal 'running-in' positions on each platform. The east end retaining walls were painted white, which at first gave an unaccustomed brightness. By the early 1970s this paint was flaking and discoloured, and the whole station looked neglected. The run-down atmosphere persisted as the passenger emerged onto Nile Street, a desperately uninviting shopping street.

Since re-opening for Metro service on 14 November 1982, North Shields has looked much tidier. A new deck concourse entrance building, new ramps, and tall platform lamps have been erected. The 1960s awnings have been retained, but a redundant section of the trainshed wall has gone. A bay platform has been added to the western end of the up platform for terminating trains from St James.

Meadow Well

This station opened as Smith's Park on 14 November

A Class 101 leaves a somewhat neglected North Shields station on 24 July 1977.   *(Alan Young)*

1982 with standard Metro structures. Following widely-reported unrest in the adjacent housing estate, City Challenge funding was used to upgrade the estate as well as the station (renamed Meadow Well on 10 October 1994) which received smart new platform shelters of a hipped roof design.

Percy Main
(Newcastle & North Shields Railway)
This station opened with the line to Shields on 20 June 1839. Percy Main was a small riverside community clustered around a colliery.

The two platforms were on an embankment. Access was through the main building on the up side. This was of red brick with a slate roof, almost as tall as it was long. A flight of steps led from the street to a door at first-floor level. Further steps led to the platform, where the upper storey looked stunted and undistinguished. A typical NER footbridge gave access to the down platform, where there was a timber waiting room with a pitched roof. Percy Main's LNER electric lamps and B.R. totems were removed about 1971 and tall new lamps were installed. The totems re-appeared on the new lamps, so 'corporate identity' signs never appeared.

Percy Main closed on 11 August 1980 for Metro work which involved demolition of all of the buildings and their replacement with modern simple shelters.

The B&T opened their own station at Percy Main on 28 August 1841, but it closed to passengers on 27 June 1864. It was situated immediately north of the N&NS station. In 1956 its single-storey buildings were still standing: they have since been demolished. The B&T locomotive and waggon workshops, later demoted to an engine shed, were situated some 300yd south of the bridge under the N&NS. The shed was closed and demolished in 1966.

Howdon-on-Tyne
The N&NS opened Howdon station on 18 June 1839.

The NER renamed it Howdon-on-Tyne on 1 December 1875 to avoid confusion with Howden between Selby and Hull. This is the only Coast Circle station with access from a public road level crossing.

The two platforms were west of the crossing. The main building, housing the ticket office, stood on the up side. It was a dull, two-storey brick structure with a pitched slate roof and some rendering at first-floor level on the platform side. Added to this building was a small wooden shed, which adjoined a brick and timber shelter of the rabbit hutch type. A similar shelter stood on the opposite platform. An NER footbridge spanned the tracks. For many years the station has been dwarfed by gas-holders south of the line, the remnants of the once extensive Howdon Gasworks which stretched to Willington Quay station on the Riverside Branch.

Passenger business in 1911 was relatively quiet for the Coast Circle. Housing development began north of the line after World War I, swelling the traffic.

Goods facilities were withdrawn on 7 July 1964, and passenger trains ceased on 11 August 1980 for Metro work. When it was re-opened (as plain Howdon) on 14 November 1982, all of the buildings and the up platform had been demolished. The platforms are now staggered either side of the crossing, with simple shelters. The footbridge has been re-erected at Goathland on the North Yorkshire Moors Railway.

Hadrian Road
Belatedly providing alternative facilities for the closed Point Pleasant station on the Riverside Branch, Hadrian Road opened on 14 November 1982. It has standard passenger shelters. This was one of the locations which had been proposed for a new station (Rosehill) before World War II. Use of this station is light, since much of the industry it was intended to serve closed in the late 1970s and early 1980s.

A Metro Cammell set accelerates away from Percy Main towards the coast on 24 July 1977. *(Alan Young)*

The exterior of Percy Main in 1977. *(Alan Young)*

A Newcastle train enters Howdon on Tyne on 27 July 1979. The buildings were demolished when the Metro took over but the footbridge found a new home at Goathland on the North York Moors Railway. *(Alan Young)*

Wallsend looking towards Howdon-on-Tyne in 1959. The awnings were removed in the late 1960s. *(Stations UK)*

Wallsend

The first station to serve this town, which was then separate from Newcastle, opened on 20 June 1839. A new one on the same site was authorised in August 1884 to handle the growing traffic of commuters, shipyard workers, and shoppers. Buildings on both platforms were in red brick and of little architectural merit. A two-storey structure stood at the east end of the up platform beside the bridge over Station Road, the upper storey being at platform level. Glazed, ridged awnings fronted the buildings on both platforms. The western ends of both platforms had timber extensions.

By 1972 the awnings were removed, exposing the dull buildings, and leaving the elevated platforms looking bleak and unattractive. The station remained in this state until its closure for Metro works on 11 August 1980. It re-opened on 14 November 1982 with standard Metro shelters. There are ramps and steps to each platform, and these are connected by a ramped underpass.

Walker Gate

When opened on 19 June 1839 this station was known as Walker. It was renamed Walker Gate on 1 April 1889. In 1908 the NER rebuilt the station in a single-storey timber sports pavilion style.

Walker Gate's new main building was on the up platform. It was a long structure with a hipped slate roof. Above the booking hall window was a large gable facing the platform, while two of the door openings to the platform had smaller gables. Even a small wooden shed at the east end was treated to a frilly bargeboard and a small finial. On the down platform was a small timber building with a pitched roof. A typical NER footbridge connected the platforms. Goods and carriage sidings were located west of the platforms.

Walker Gate was adversely affected by the introduction of electric trams on neighbouring roads. 116,481 tickets were issued in 1901 but only 56,278 in 1911.

The station lost its goods facilities on 14 August 1967 and passenger trains on 11 August 1980 for Metro works. All platform buildings were dismantled, but the footbridge was salvaged for use at Pickering on the North Yorkshire Moors Railway. The station, re-opened on 14 November 1982, was almost indistinguishable from the others up to Percy Main. The Metro station is known as Walkergate. The single word name had previously been carried on the N.E. Region nameboards and on the 1970s 'corporate identity' nameplates, but the totems read Walker Gate. In British Railways timetables the two word form was preferred.

Seen in 1979, the entrance to Wallsend is neither charming nor welcoming. *(Alan Young)*

The timber building at Walker Gate dated from 1908. It resembled those on the Ponteland branch which were built about the same time.
(Alan Young)

Chillingham Road

This Metro station opened on 14 November 1982, east of Chillingham Road bridge, on the new Metro alignment. Before it opened the station was provisionally called Parsons, after the nearby engineering works. This is another station with simple buildings.

Heaton

Heaton was served by Coast Circle and main line trains. Eight years after the Newcastle Carliol Square-North Shields route, Heaton station opened with the main line on 1 July 1847 in rural surroundings immediately east of Heaton Road bridge. The widening of the shared section of route between Heaton Junction and Manors prompted the NER to rebuild the station, to the west of Heaton Road. The new facilities opened on 1 April 1887.

The new Heaton had two island platforms. The northern one (1 and 2) served down and up main lines respectively, and the southern one (3 and 4) down and up Coast Circle trains. The outer down line swerved around platform 1, making a speed restriction necessary. The platforms were sheltered by long, ridged awnings. Sturdy iron columns and spandrels with the Star of David motif supported them. Elswick, opened on the Carlisle line in 1889, had almost identical awnings.

The booking hall and other offices were in a long, timber building slung across all four tracks approximately mid-way along the station, from which wide ramps descended under the awnings. A small booking office stood on the Heaton Road overbridge above platforms 3 and 4, to issue local tickets.

In 1974 the platforms were stripped of their awnings, and a small metal passenger shelter, of the type then in vogue, was placed on platforms 3 and 4. The booking hall survived the carnage. With the prospect of Metro stations nearby at Chillingham Road and Byker, Heaton was closed on 11 August 1980. Demolition was rapid, with nothing left to see by the end of that year apart from the gaps where the platforms had stood. By 1998 the former down main line had been removed, whilst the former up slow still curved around the platform site.

Byker

Opened on 14 November 1982 this deck concourse station is in a cutting, with stairs and ramps down to platform level. There is a newsagent's kiosk in the ticketing area.

Monument

This is the largest, most heavily used station on the Metro system, and its route focus. It has four access points, each with stairs down to concourse level. There is also a lift from the Eldon Square entrance, and lifts and escalators to all levels in Monument Mall. A travel centre is in the concourse ticketing area. Escalators and lifts descend from the concourse to the first level north-south and lower level east-west platforms. Stairs and a lift also connect the two pairs of platforms. It opened on 15 November 1981.

St James

This underground terminus opened on 14 November 1982, close to Newcastle United football ground and Gallowgate coach station. Access to the platforms involves a long descent by stairs, escalators, or lift.

Haymarket

At its opening on 11 August 1980 this was the Metro's southern terminus. The circular entrance building contains the concourse, ticket machines, a travel centre, and two newsagents. Access to the underground island platform is by stairs, lifts, and escalator. The station is heavily used, serving the busiest shopping areas, the two universities, and the Civic Centre.

The booking hall and offices at Heaton were in this unpretentious wooden building slung across the four tracks. The entrance on North View was photographed on 31 December 1972. *(Alan Young)*

Seen from Heaton Road Bridge in 1973, the station retained its full range of buildings and awnings dating from 1887. *(Alan Young)*

By December 1974, the platforms were bare apart from a small metal 'bus shelter' for coast line passengers, but nothing on the main line. *(Alan Young)*

The Riverside Branch

The 16.43 to Tynemouth does brisk business at Carville on 6 June 1972. *(Alan Young)*

The 6½ mile branch (actually a loop, rather than a branch) was strikingly indirect when compared with the Coast Circle route between Manors and Percy Main. A journey between these two stations via Wallsend was two miles shorter, and up to eleven minutes faster, than the Carville detour. The Byker to Carville section followed the meandering River Tyne. It included tight curves through Byker, and at St Anthonys where a 10mph speed restriction was enforced. The remainder ran almost parallel to the Wallsend line for two miles, and for much of this distance the lines were in sight of each other.

The route was chosen to serve rapidly growing communities along the north bank of the River Tyne which the direct North Shields line had missed. When the Riverside Branch opened on 1 May 1879 stations were provided at St Peters, St Anthonys, Low Walker (Walker from 13 May 1889), Carville, and Willington Quay. Byker and Point Pleasant opened for advertised passenger services in 1901 and 1902 respectively.

Let us take a journey (direct from Newcastle) in the early 1960s. This begins on the Wallsend line through Manors (East) and across Ouseburn viaduct. Soon after the viaduct, at Riverside Junction signal box, the branch leaves the Wallsend route, curving sharply to the right. The disused platforms of **Byker** (1½ miles) are immediate after

the junction, followed by the 140yd Byker Tunnel under Shields Road. The tight curve causes the wheel flanges to emit a deafening screech, amplified within the tunnel. A cutting with massive retaining walls follows, in which there is a steep descent, easing off at a tight curve to the left, before **St Peters** (2½ miles). From St Peters to **St Anthonys** (3¼ miles) there is a superb view of the River Tyne, immediately to the right, and across the river to the dereliction of Felling Shore. The Tyne's change of direction is followed by the railway from St Anthonys, where a sharp left curve begins at the site of the recently demolished station. Travelling north-eastwards now, we enter the 182yd Walker Tunnel. Factories and sidings to our right herald our arrival at **Walker** (4¼ miles). Until Carville there is an uninterrupted view of shipyards and factories to the right of the line, with glimpses of the river and Hebburn beyond. A tight curve to the right and a level crossing brings us to **Carville** (5¾ miles). Here the platform is crowded with workers from Wallsend shipyard. Passing more industries and sidings on the right, **Point Pleasant** (6½ miles) is entered after a fairly straight ¾ mile stretch. Hardly living up to its name, Point Pleasant station is overshadowed by the massive black walls of Wallsend Slipway. The highlight of the journey to Willington Quay is a substantial bridge over the Wallsend Burn (o

Willington Gut) with a fine view of the viaduct on the Wallsend route to the north. Soon, Howdon Gasworks dominates the view to the left, towering above **Willington Quay** (7 miles). The Wallsend line comes back into view, and the routes converge just before **Percy Main** station (8 miles from Central via Riverside).

Stations
The Riverside station buildings were of little architectural merit and more uniform than those on the Coast Circle. Each had two side-platforms. The main building at the five original stations – St Peters, St Anthonys, Walker, Carville, and Willington Quay – was a single storey brick structure with a veranda between twin pavilions. Small, dignified brick shelters with a central door and two windows were provided on the other platform.

Before looking at each station in turn, standardised features found at Riverside stations are worth mentioning. From 1970, in common with many stations in the Newcastle Division, every Riverside station received tall vandal-proof electric lamps. These replaced LNER swans-neck lamps (with an exposed bulb, rather than with a mint imperial lampshade) which remained only at the closed Byker station. Good lighting was essential, since in December and January Riverside stations had no train service in daylight hours.

Signposting at Riverside stations in the British Railways era consisted of a hand-painted wooden nameboard in tangerine on each platform. Because of the line's uncertain future, vitreous enamel nameboards and later 'corporate identity' nameplates were not installed. Until shortly before

closure, Walker and Carville each had a small LNER nameplate fixed to the wall of the booking hall.

Byker
Byker was a late addition. Trains made unadvertised calls from 1884 but official opening was on 1 March 1901. Goods facilities were not provided.

The site was immediately beyond the junction with the Coast Circle, tucked behind the shopping street of Shields Road. Its down platform ramp was only a foot wide where it squeezed into the gap between the down Riverside and the up Coast lines, sharing the constricted site with Riverside Junction signal box. The buildings were simpler than at the earlier stations, consisting of a waiting shelter on each platform and a small booking office south of the up platform. A footbridge connected the platforms.

Byker was administratively an annexe to Heaton, so passenger bookings for most of its life were credited to Heaton. This subordinate status, and its former role as a workmen's 'halt' may explain why the Ordnance Survey 1:2 500 map of 1913 referred to it as Byker Platform. Passenger use was limited by the proximity of Heaton station, with its vastly superior service, and the frequent trams, buses, and trolley buses on Shields Road. The obscure site, approached from an inconspicuous street off Shields Road, and inaccessibility from the north also reduced its traffic. With these factors loaded against it, Byker closed on 5 April 1954.

A quarter-century after closure Byker station retained both platforms, lamp-posts, and nameboard stanchions. However, the site is now landfilled.

The remains of Byker Station, closed ten years earlier, photographed from a passing main line train on 19 September 1964.
(Alan Young)

St Peters

This station opened on 1 May 1879, serving a developing industrial and residential area. The main twin-pavilion single-storey brick structure stood on the down platform. The north-west end pavilion had a small square bay with its own small gable. A subway connected the platforms.

By 1972 no buildings remained on the up platform. The other platform had been narrowed by the encroachment of Shepherd's Scrapyard onto the site, and was backed by an unsightly concrete wall. A small hut – the ticket office – stood at the west end of the down platform. Passengers on the platforms therefore had no protection against the weather, but they could shelter in the subway and study the graffiti on the white glazed brick walls.

St Peters had the honour of a visit by HM Queen Elizabeth, the Queen Mother, in 1961, when she alighted to launch a ship. As a token gesture, the platform she used was decorated. The other was hidden from view by a strategically parked train!

Passenger use declined steadily, measured either by tickets issued or those collected. By 1972 St Peters booked fewer passengers than any other staffed station in the Newcastle Division, with the exception of Chathill.

On 23 July 1973 the station closed to passengers. Although goods facilities had been withdrawn on 31 October 1966, sidings serving the scrapyard remained in use until 25 September 1987; the rest of the line to Percy Main had closed completely by then. In 1979, the station remained almost unchanged since closure, complete with a nameboard, but minus the lamps and ticket hut. By 1998 the rails had gone and the site had been landscaped.

A reminder that staff at St Peters once had crowds to control. *(Alan Young)*

St Peters looking towards St Anthonys in 1959. Previously there had been an awning between the two projecting gables. *(Stations UK)*

St Anthonys

This station was on a narrow ledge overlooking the River Tyne. It opened with the line on 1 May 1879. No goods facilities were provided. The main buildings on the down platform were very similar to those at St Peters. A subway connected the platforms.

Passengers deserted the station in the 1950s, and, with the line's lowest figures both for issue and collection of tickets, St Anthonys closed on 12 September 1960. There was no catchment area to the south and east, owing to the closeness of the river. Buses and trolley-buses along Walker Road served the residential area north of the station far better than the trains could.

St Anthonys was demolished by 1963. A short stretch of the trackbed through the site, including a skew-arch bridge immediately to the east, is now within Riverside Park and is a cycle path.

Walker

From opening on 1 May 1879 until 13 May 1889 this station was called Low Walker. The standard main building with an awning between the pavilions stood on the down platform. The awning had disappeared by 1959. At the north end of the platform was the station house, two-storey and brick-built, without decoration. A small conservatory attached to the station house may have been a later addition. A brick lock-up stood south of the group of buildings. Beyond the southern end of the platform was a typical brick-based NER signal box with a hipped roof. This was in place until the line closed to passengers. The up platform brick-built waiting room was also of the standard Riverside type. Passengers crossed the line by a subway.

Walker served shipyards and other factories east of the line, but the western side was somewhat sparsely built-up. Being close to Walker Road with its trams, and later buses and trolley-buses, there was fierce competition for passengers, yet the station was reasonably busy. In 1939 it booked more passengers than any other Riverside Branch station. Goods services lasted until 14 August 1967.

The full complement of buildings remained until closure, on 23 July 1973. In 1979 only the station house and the brick lock-up remained, and the up platform alone had rails in place. The remaining track was removed after goods services ceased between St Peters and Carville in April 1987. By 1998 the site had been cleared and was used as a scrapyard.

Carville

Almost adjacent to Wallsend was Carville, which opened with the Riverside Branch on 1 May 1879. The single-storey main building was at the west end of the down platform. This resembled its neighbours at the other original stations but was more elaborate. The frontage had a large central gable over the entrance, with decorative woodwork under the gable and a finial above. The pitched roof-line of the twin pavilions on the platform side ended in half-hipped gables on the frontage. At the east end of the building, looking like an afterthought, was a further section which reversed the roof details of the pavilions, with a half-hipped end facing the platform and a gable end on the frontage.

Because the platforms were built on a tight curve and the building was straight and parallel to the road it fronted, the west end of the platform was progressively wider towards the ramp. Conversely, at the eastern end of the main building, the additional section under a half-hipped roof was recessed, so as not to make the platform dangerously narrow. On the platform, a glazed waiting room with a lean-to roof stretched between the pavilions, and above its central entrance on the platform side was a small gable. The two pavilion gables were decorated with simple wooden finials and pendants, which survived until closure. On the same side of the tracks beyond the level crossing was a tall brick-built NER signal box with a pitched roof, accompanied by a row of railway cottages. The up platform had a wooden waiting shelter towards its west end.

A more ambitious main building design, with an arched portico, a small tower, and white glazed interior was intended for Carville station but was never built. It was probably thought extravagant in such an industrial environment.

Despite its proximity to Wallsend station, Carville was not starved of passengers. In the closing years of the branch, Carville was its busiest station, conveniently situated at the entrance to Wallsend Shipyard. When the siren announced the end of the afternoon shift, hundreds of men poured out of the premises, many of them onto the platforms at Carville; the station, silent during the day, was crowded for a few minutes.

The main building survived until closure on 23 July 1973, though only the western end of the glazed waiting room was intact. If they had the inclination, passengers could admire a display of potted plants on the south-facing waiting room window ledge. There were no buildings on the up platform at the time of closure.

Carville had goods facilities until 11 July 1966 (known as Wallsend from 1 December 1913: Wallsend passenger station had no goods facilities). After Carville closed to passengers, a track remained in place until at least April 1987, terminating at Swan Hunter's Wallsend Shipyard.

In 1979 the station was still largely intact. The 'British Railways Carville' enamel sign remained on the exterior wall, and the up platform nameboard had not been removed. Being wooden and faded to the point of illegibility it was not a collector's item! The lower half of the signal box was in place, still bearing its nameplate.

By 1998 there was little evidence that there had ever been a station at Carville. The site of the main building was occupied by a petrol station. The base of the signal box had been converted into a store. However, the railway cottages were still standing.

St Anthonys looking towards Newcastle. Entrances to the subway are just beyond the buildings. *(Stations UK)*

Walker on 4 July 1973, a fortnight before closure. The twin pavilion building was still in use as booking office and station house. *(Alan Young)*

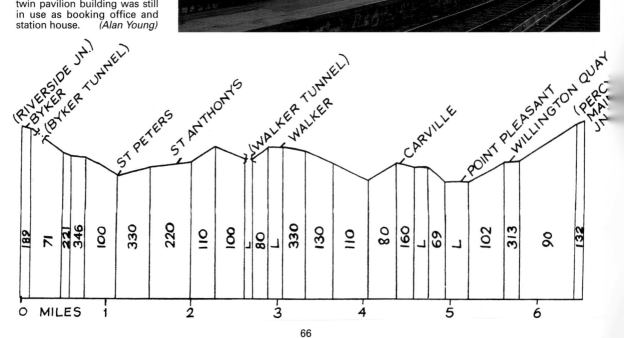

The exterior of Carville on 8 July 1973, a fortnight before closure. *(Alan Young)*

Point Pleasant

It is uncertain when Point Pleasant was built but, before it became a public station on 1 January 1902, it had an unadvertised workmen's service. Its humble origins were reflected in the simple wooden shelters which survived until the 1960s.

The platforms were linked by a standard NER iron lattice footbridge, the only elegant feature of this station. On the down platform, a timber shed contained the waiting room and booking office. Beyond the west end of this platform was a signal box. The up platform had an open waiting shelter with its slanting roof carried upwards towards the track as an awning, a further waiting room, also of timber construction, and another shed which ended up tilting towards the track at about 10deg. In March 1963 an *Evening Chronicle* reporter visiting the station was shocked by its dereliction, the holes in the roof, the handless clock, and the absence of staff to interview. 'The station that belies its name' aptly described Point Pleasant!

In its last years, Point Pleasant lost its footbridge. It retained only a tiny wooden ticket office on the down platform and a little brick shed on the up side. There was no provision for passenger comfort: shipyard workers were presumably thought to be tough specimens who could cope with the absence of seats, decent shelters, or toilets! Even in the closing weeks of train services, so many passengers crowded the platforms that it would have been impractical to provide enough seats. Immaculate wooden nameboards graced each platform at closure, resplendent in their tangerine paint, free from graffiti.

Figures for passenger bookings and tickets collected show that, despite meagre facilities, Point Pleasant became one of the busier stations on the branch. In 1957 the numbers of tickets collected, at almost 159,000, was remarkable. Its nearest rival, Carville, collected just over 104,000. Although traffic declined through the 1960s, Point Pleasant continued to serve Wallsend Slipway, Cleland's Shipyard, and North Eastern Marine.

After closure, the platforms remained until at least 1979, but the rails had been removed. By 1998 nothing was left. The site was used for industrial purposes and car parking.

Willington Quay

This station opened on 1 May 1879. On the up platform was a standard twin-pavilion building, with a lean-to awning supported by five pillars. The down platform had a brick waiting room like that at Walker. An NER footbridge was provided. At the west end of the down platform was a brick-built NER signal box, with a hipped roof.

Although reasonably busy before World War II, passenger traffic was light in later years, with only a little more trade than St Peters in its last full year of operation. The closeness of Howdon-on-Tyne with its frequent train service tempted passengers away from the delights of Willington Quay.

Goods facilities were withdrawn from 2 October 1967, and passenger closure took place on 23 July 1973. The only building surviving at closure was one pavilion of the main building (with a hole in the roof) and a fragment of the adjacent shelter. The footbridge was still in place.

By 31 May 1978 the last goods trains had passed through the station. The rails were lifted by July 1979 but the platforms remained. By 1987 the site had been cleared.

Staffed or unstaffed stations?

One book describing the Riverside branch in its closing years refers to the stations as 'sordid, vandalised, unstaffed halts'. Neglected they certainly were. However, the Riverside stations were *officially* staffed, but for most of the day no-one was on duty: Willington Quay appeared derelict and the 'Tickets' signs on the diminutive cabins at St Peters and Point Pleasant would not be taken seriously. But several minutes before trains arrived in mornings and late-afternoons, a railway employee would unlock these buildings and issue tickets. Technically staff attended every passenger!

Point Pleasant looking west in 1959. *(Stations UK)*

At least 30 customers are standing on the down platform or squatting uncomfortably in the weeds, as they wait at Point Pleasant for the 16.46 to Tynemouth on 13 July 1973. *(Alan Young)*

Willington Quay in 1959 looking towards Point Pleasant. Howdon-on-Tyne was only 500 yards away. *(Stations UK)*

Timetables

The timetable history of the Riverside line is remarkable.

In August 1887 the service operated in both directions on weekdays at approximately two-hourly intervals, increasing by 1910 to an hourly service every day. *Bradshaw* of July 1938 shows an hourly service supplemented by extra trains on weekday mornings, in the late-afternoon rush-hour on Mondays to Fridays, and at lunchtime on Saturdays, when shipyards closed for the weekend. One train ran each way on Sunday morning. By July 1943 several daytime services had been withdrawn, as had the Sunday trains.

In the winter of 1948-49 the Riverside service was considerably reduced, catering only for the shipyard commuter traffic. Two weekday trains operated to Newcastle by the direct route – one in the morning and the other in early afternoon – and four in the reverse direction – two in the morning, one at lunchtime, and one in the evening. Winter 1953-54 saw a further reduction to one weekday train to Newcastle direct, and only three in the opposite direction.

The timetable effective from June 1955 provided a more generous and complex weekday service. Simplification of the timetable followed, and by the summer of 1958 there were only eleven Riverside train columns in the passenger timetable as against nineteen in the summer of 1955. However, in the summer of 1961 the timetable reached new heights of complexity. The Tuesdays and Thursdays working to West Monkseaton from Newcastle via Riverside operated on the evenings in which late shifts were worked at the shipyards, but did not appear in the public timetables after winter 1961-62.

A series of simplifications followed, and in October 1970 the service achieved its final austerity of Monday to Friday 06.58 and 16.24 down workings from Newcastle, and 06.20 and 0.745 up workings from Newcastle via Benton, with another train starting its advertised journey at 16.40 from Willington Quay. An unadvertised train also operated on Tuesdays, Wednesdays, and Thursdays for shipyard overtime workers. It ran empty from Newcastle at 18.19 arriving at St Peters at 18.26, where passengers could join before its departure at 18.32. It then called at all stations to West Monkseaton before returning empty to Gosforth car sheds.

Riverside Branch passenger figures

Since the stations were staffed, figures are available for tickets booked and collected. Detailed analysis would show a connection between the fortunes of the individual stations and the prosperity of the shipyards they served.

The passenger booking figures for 1939 show the following ranking of Riverside branch stations:

Walker	52,452
Willington Quay	35,145
St Anthonys	22,702
St Peters	18,050
Carville	17,884
Point Pleasant	15,145

(Byker bookings were credited to Heaton)

By World War II the stations served workplaces rather than homes, and many of the passengers will have obtained return tickets at their home station; therefore numbers of outward halves of tickets collected at Riverside stations is a better guide to station use than tickets issued.

By the mid-1950s Byker had closed, and St Anthonys, which was to close in 1960, had slumped

Willington Quay looking towards Newcastle on 13 July 1973.   (Alan Young)

Table 55 **NEWCASTLE and TYNEMOUTH via RIVERSIDE**
(Electric Trains) (Second Class Only) 1961

WEEKDAYS ONLY

Miles						SO		FO		FO		FSX		FSX		TThO
			am	To Newcastle (arr 8.29 am) (Table 54)	am	To West Monkseaton (arr 12.37 pm) (Table 54)	noon	To West Monkseaton (arr 5.0 pm) (Table 54)	pm	To Longbenton (arr 5.27 pm) (Table 54)	pm	To West Monkseaton (arr 5.32 pm) (Table 54)	pm	To Longbenton (arr 5.57 pm) (Table 54)	pm	To West Monkseaton (arr 8.54 pm) (Table 54)	pm
—	**NEWCASTLE**	dep	6 54		....		12 0		....		4 31		....		5 4		8 16
½	Manors	,,	6 56		..		12 2		..		4 33		..		5 6		8 18
2½	St. Peters	,,	7 0		7 35		12 6		....		4 40		....		5 10		8 22
4¼	Walker	,,	7 6		7 40		12 12		4 32		4 47		5 4		5 18		8 30
5¾	Carville	,,	7 9		7 43		12 15		4 36		4 50		5 8		5 22		8 33
6½	Point Pleasant	,,	7 12		7 45		12 17		4 40		4 54		5 12		5 26		8 35
7	Willington Quay	,,	7 14		7 47		12 19		4 42		4 56		5 14		5 28		8 37
8	Percy Main	,,	7 17		7 50		12 22		4 45		4 59		5 17		5 31		8 40
9¼	North Shields	,,	7 20		7 52		12 25		4 48		5 2		5 20		5 34		8 42
10¼	**TYNEMOUTH**	arr	7 23		7 55		12 28		4 51		5 6		5 23		5 37		8 45

WEEKDAYS ONLY

Miles					SX		SX	FO	FSX		SX
			From Longbenton (dep 6.32 am) (Table 54)	am	am	From Monkseaton (dep 8.18 am.) (Table 54)	am	pm	pm	From Newcastle (dep 5.0 pm) (Table 54)	pm
—	**TYNEMOUTH**	dep		6 56	7 8		8 27	....	....		5 25
1	North Shields	,,		7 0	7 11		8 30	..	..		5 28
2¼	Percy Main	,,		7 3	7 14		8 33	....	....		5 31
3¼	Willington Quay	,,		7 5	7 16		8 35	4 40	5 10		5 33
3¾	Point Pleasant	,,		7 7	7 18		8 38	4 44	5 13		5 35
4½	Carville	,,		7 10	7 21		8 40	4 47	5 16		5 37
6	Walker	,,		7 14	7 24		8 43	4 51	5 20		5 40
7¾	St. Peters	,,		7 18	7 29		8 49	4 55	5 24		5 45
9¾	Manors	,,		—	7 34		8 54	5 0	5 29		5 50
10¼	**NEWCASTLE**	arr		....	7 37		8 57	5 3	5 32		5 53

For complete service of trains between Newcastle, Percy Main, North Shields and Tynemouth, see Table 54.
For other trains between Newcastle and Manors, see Tables 3 and 54

FO—Fridays only. **FSX**—Fridays and Saturdays excepted. | **SO**—Saturdays only. **SX**—Saturdays excepted. | **TThO**—Tuesdays and Thursdays only.

to the bottom of the list. Willington Quay's traffic had fallen markedly between 1939 and 1957, while Carville and Point Pleasant stations had grown in importance.

Passenger bookings at Riverside Branch stations:

	1911	1939	1957	1967	1972
Byker	28,741	no data	——	——	——
St Peters	37,111	18,050	11,866	4,919	1,868
St Anthonys	11,283	22,702	11,408	——	——
Walker	37,247	52,452	34,611	23,773	18,133
Carville	29,780	17,884	39,197	18,051	28,639
Point Pleasant	24,934	5,145	37,217	15,536	19,184
Willington Quay	30,684	35,145	16,718	7,706	4,722

Tickets collected at Riverside Branch stations:

	1957	1962	1967	1971	1972
Byker	——	——	——	——	——
St Peters	22,330	15,746	12,533	6,644	4,803
St Anthonys	10,052	——	——	——	——
Walker	75,726	55,935	37,790	25,395	17,074
Carville	104,458	41,056	59,500	34,190	24,433
Point Pleasant	158,927	86,710	55,970	30,980	20,263
Willington Quay	36,764	30,376	20,589	12,641	7,535

The figures for 1972, the final full calendar-year of operation, emphasise that Walker, Carville and Point Pleasant served the shipyards. Willington Quay was reasonably well placed to serve Cleland's Shipyard, but it was better served by Point Pleasant. Carville's total was the greatest, but its 28,639 bookings shrink almost to insignificance against nearby Wallsend's 397,734.

Run-down and closure

After World War II, expenses were reduced by limiting the service to Monday-Saturday peak hours, and Byker and St Anthonys were closed in 1954 and 1960 respectively. Further economies, shared with the main Coast Circle, involved the replacement of electric trains by diesel multiple units in 1967.

Closure was recommended in *The Reshaping of British Railways* (Beeching Report). Revealing the implications of the proposals for the North East, Newcastle *Evening Chronicle* of 27 March 1963 had a feature on the Riverside Branch. This stressed the importance of the line to users and described a journey by the 7.08 from Tynemouth. The reporter's references to Point Pleasant were less than complimentary.

Many other lines and stations did close soon after the Report's publication, but the Riverside was reprieved in 1964 pending construction of a road between Hadrian Road, Wallsend, and Bewicke Road, Willington Quay. Eventually, in 1971, after reviewing Tyneside's transport requirements, the PTE decided not to subsidise the Riverside Branch under the 1968 Transport Act. In mid-1972, the road linking Carville, Point Pleasant, and Willington Quay was built, and closure of the line was again recommended. On 17 April 1973 consent was given on the understanding that replacement bus licences would be obtained by 23 July 1973. It was acknowledged that a moderate amount of hardship would be caused to a small number of passengers owing to increased journey time and road congestion, especially to users of St Peters and Walker stations.

Annual costs of the Riverside service were stated at £100,000 against earnings of only £15,000. It was claimed that, within one year of closure, there would be a saving of £21,000. While other marginal lines had been singled, the Riverside had double track throughout its length and stations were staffed. In November 1972 the Tyneside Metropolitan Railway Bill confirmed that most of the Coast Circle was to be included in a rapid light transit system but the Riverside would be abandoned. In July 1973 only a few days separated Royal Assent to the Bill and closure of the Riverside Branch.

It was fitting that the Riverside Branch had no special final train for railway enthusiasts. Instead they had to decide which train was the final one! The 16.24 from Newcastle (direct) was the last over the entire branch, whilst the 16.40 starting from Willington Quay was the last train on Riverside metals. Few people were there to pay their last respects. A hand-chalked notice under the remains of the awning at Willington Quay announced the closure: *'No more waiting here after today.'*

Seaton Sluice and the Collywell Bay Branch

The coastal village of Seaton Sluice developed as a port in the 17th Century. Originally known as Hartley Harbour, its present name comes from the sluice gates installed across the harbour in 1690 to trap water at high tide. These were opened at low tide to flush out silt. As early as 1738 Seaton Sluice had a waggonway to Hartley Colliery, built by the Delaval family, but the Avenue Branch passenger trains between Hartley and Monkseaton by-passed the village. For a short time, between 1847 and 1852, a limited passenger train service operated along the waggonway/mineral line, between Seaton Sluice and Hartley.

The NER recognised the potential for commuter traffic if housing development were encouraged by an electrified branch from Monkseaton. Shortly after electrification of the Coast Circle, a construction contract was agreed on 14 November 1912 with C.M. Skinner for a two-mile line to Seaton Sluice. It was to leave the Avenue Branch about a mile north of Monkseaton station and this section of the Avenue Branch would be increased to double track. The terminus was to be called Collywell Bay; this name was considered more attractive than Seaton Sluice! An intermediate station was planned at Brierdene, where an elaborate wooden building was to be constructed.

In May 1913 Lord Hastings signed an Agreement allowing the NER to build the line over his land of which he was to sell 21 1/2 acres at £40 per acre. The NER expected to introduce a passenger service at the beginning of November 1914. Construction was well advanced when World War I broke out. House building in the area ceased, and the newly-laid tracks were removed for use on the battlefields. However a single track was restored for use by a naval coastal defence gun, mounted on a specially built railway waggon.

After the War the local council expected the line to be completed. The LNER reviewed the project in 1924 but did not proceed because little housing development had taken place at Seaton Sluice. The Collywell Bay line was finally abandoned by an Agreement between the LNER and Lord Hastings on 1 December 1931, but the stations were allowed to remain in place. Track dismantling was under way by the spring of 1931.

Collywell Bay station was built, but it never saw a passenger train. Its platforms were still in place in 1964, serving as a compound for livestock. Until the 1960s the trackbed of the branch remained, as well as the abutments of a railway overbridge beside Hartley Lane in Seaton Sluice, and the site of Brierdene station.

Killingworth – Gosforth Park Light Railway
The NER deposited plans with Parliament for this railway on 30 November 1895, but nothing came of the scheme. Gosforth Park did receive a railway of sorts, when a double-track Newcastle Corporation tramway opened in 1921, officially known as the Gosforth Park Light Railway. For a mile-and-a-half it had a dedicated route through the park, with a four track 'station' close to the race course. The line closed in 1948, but long after its abandonment, its route through Gosforth Park could be followed.

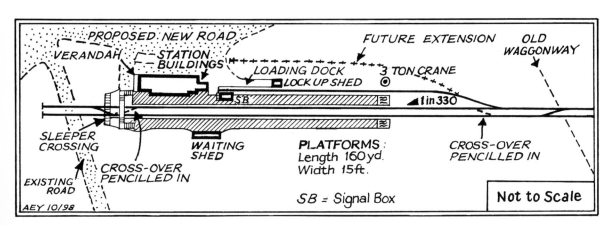

PROPOSED STATION AT COLLYWELL BAY 1913

Tyne Commission Quay

The last passenger train at Tyne Commission Quay on 2 May 1970. 'The Norseman' headboard recalls the through train to Kings Cross which used to connect with the steamer from Bergen.
(Trevor Ermel)

The boat trains served the Norwegian ships from Tyne Commission Quay. At that time the Danish ships of DFDS (The United Steamship Company) sailed from Newcastle Quayside. Nowadays the much larger vessels of DFDS sail from Tyne Commission Quay.

The 'Parkeston' is seen leaving Newcastle Quayside for Esbjerg in August 1960. Built in 1925, the 2,762 ton 'Parkeston' was the first North Sea passenger ferry to be diesel powered. It was withdrawn in 1964 but survived as a workers' accommodation ship in Oslo until 1975. *(Peter Sunderland)*

The summer 1958 timetable. On some days the Fred Olsen sailing, to Kristiansand and Oslo, and the Bergen Line, to Stavanger and Bergen, were only 30 minutes apart allowing one train to connect with both ships.

Table 65 NEWCASTLE and TYNE COMMISSION QUAY
(BERGEN LINE and FRED OLSEN LINE BOAT TRAINS)

Miles		WEEKDAYS										
		H	D L	D SO	D T	G	G	D G				
	2 London (King's Cross) .. dep	am 9 5	am 9 8	am 9 40	am 9 40			am 10 40				
—	NEWCASTLE .... dep	pm 1 28	pm 2 2	pm 2 22	pm 2 42	pm 3 8	pm 3 45	pm 4 25				
8¼	TYNE COMMISSION QUAY .... arr	2 3	2 32	2 52	3 12	3 38	4 15	4 55				

Miles		WEEKDAYS									
		B	D C	D G	D F	M A	D J	D SO	J	SO	
	TYNE COMMISSION QUAY .... dep	am 8 6	am 8 40	am 8 55	am 8 55	am 9 10	am 10 11	pm 12 10	pm 12 30	pm 12 35	
8¼	NEWCASTLE .... arr	8 43	9 10	9 24	9 24	9 41	11 25	12 40	1 5	1 10	
	2 London (King's Cross) .. arr	pm 2 15	pm 3 7	pm 3 3	pm 3 3	pm 3 22	pm 5 22	pm 5 40			

A—Friday 12th September only.
B—Runs Mondays, Wednesdays, Thursdays and Fridays also Saturdays until 30th August inclusive. Conveys through carriage to Edinburgh (Waverley).
C—Runs Wednesdays and Thursdays until 4th September and also on Monday 8th and Thursday 11th September.
D—Through carriages between King's Cross and Tyne Commission Quay.

F—Runs Mondays and Fridays until 5th September and also on Wednesday 10th and Friday 12th September.
G—Saturdays only. Not after 30th August.
H—Runs Mondays, Wednesdays, Thursdays and Fridays also on Friday 12th September.
J—Mondays only. Runs 23rd June to 1st September only.

L—Runs on Mondays 23rd June to 8th September; Thursdays until 28th September.
M—Runs Monday 8th September only.
SO—Saturdays Only.
T—Runs Mondays until 25th August, Wednesdays until 27th August, also on Wednesday 10th, Thursdays 4th and 11th and Friday 12th September.

For full particulars of sailings from Tyne Commission Quay see pages 44 to 46.

Ponteland, Darras Hall and Beyond

Ponteland 1963. Passenger trains had finished some 34 years earlier but there was still goods traffic until 1969. *(Stations UK)*

Although the area north west of the Coast Circle line had waggonways connecting collieries with the River Tyne, it was not until 1905 that a passenger railway was constructed to link the large village of Ponteland with Gosforth. The line was constructed under the Light Railways Act of 1896, which enabled the network to extend into parts of the country where traffic potential was limited, but where economic growth might be stimulated and isolated communities could benefit from better access. Light Railways had more relaxed regulations and signalling arrangements and could be built more cheaply.

Construction began in 1900. The route was through gently undulating countryside beyond the main built-up area, so earthworks were relatively light. There were several level crossings over public roads, but major roads and mineral lines were crossed by bridges. The line was opened to goods on 1 March 1905 and passengers on 1 June 1905.

It had been the intention to electrify the route as an extension to the Coast Circle service. An NER map of 1904 apparently showed the line as already electrified, with a sub-station at Kenton, and passenger stations at Coxlodge, Fawdon, Kenton, Woolsington, Callerton, and Ponteland. However electrification was not carried out except to allow access to Gosforth Car Sheds from 1923. Stations

were actually opened at West Gosforth, Coxlodge, Kenton, Callerton, and Ponteland. The passenger service was operated by steam autocars (push-pull sets) making ten daily runs (four on Sundays) between South Gosforth and Ponteland, taking twenty minutes for the journey. By June 1920 the Sunday trains had been withdrawn.

In November 1908 the NER deposited plans with Parliament for a 1¼ mile extension to Darras Hall, under the name of the Little Callerton Railway. Unlike the parent branch to Ponteland, the route to Darras Hall was not a Light Railway. The extension was to serve a residential area where development was only just beginning. In 1907 Darras Hall Estate began when a group of Newcastle businessmen bought land south west of Ponteland, with the aim of creating a 'garden city' for professional and managerial residents. The railway gained Parliamentary approval in 1909, and the Estate entered into an Agreement with the NER on 18 October 1910 for railway access. The single track was largely on an embankment, but space was allowed for doubling when traffic warranted it. Goods services started on 27 September 1913, and the first passenger trains rolled into the pretty little timber station on 1 October 1913. Trains from South Gosforth to Darras Hall had to reverse at Ponteland: a simple manoeuvre for the 'autocars'.

The Darras Hall extension was not a success. The Estate grew slowly, and its layout, consisting of a loose grid of roads and low density detached housing on plots of at least 1/6 acre, limited the number of potential passengers. The Trust Deeds permitted no industrial development, apart from the NER goods yard. By June 1920 only three trains per day served Darras Hall. This undoubtedly deterred potential passengers for Newcastle, who had the additional inconvenience of changing trains at South Gosforth.

Beyond Darras Hall, for a short time, the Wallridge Mineral Railway stretched ten miles north-westwards into the Northumberland countryside. Coal had been discovered early in the 20th Century at Kirkheaton, and land was leased from Dissington Estate for building a single-track mineral railway. The colliery provided employment for 100 men. Opened as far as Kirkheaton Colliery in 1921, the line's motive power was an ex-Glasgow & South Western Railway 0-6-0. Six trucks, two carriages for workmen, and a guard's van were bought for use on the line. Between 1921 and 1929 a passenger service was operated for miners. In about 1930 the colliery and railway closed, owing to problems related to labour and housing, the decline in demand for coal during the depression, and inadequate geological surveys of the coal resources. The track had been lifted by 1948, but its route can still be followed.

The Ponteland line, after a promising start, lost passengers to the more convenient buses operated by Newcastle Corporation, which also served Darras Hall. Direct bus routes operated between Kenton, Gosforth, and Newcastle. Sentinel Steam Cars replaced the autocars in the late-1920s running through to Newcastle Central, but they failed to revive passenger traffic. The service was withdrawn on 17 June 1929. The LNER had itself authorised the purchase of two buses to replace the trains, but this plan was overtaken by their investment in bus undertakings instead.

Parcels handling facilities were withdrawn on 5 January 1935, but goods continued. From time to time the branch served as a quiet retreat where the Royal Train could stop overnight. Darras Hall closed to all traffic on 2 August 1954. In the 1960s Ponteland and Callerton were remote backwaters where redundant Coast Circle electric stock was stored. Ponteland lost its goods service on 14 August 1967, and the tracks were removed beyond Prestwick ICI Siding, north of Callerton. This facility closed on 6 March 1989, but the remaining line has been incorporated into the Metro.

Between the wars, and into the 1950s and 1960s, many houses were built close to the line, whilst Newcastle Airport, close to Callerton station, grew steadily in importance. As road congestion grew, the railway's potential was wasted on small amounts of goods traffic. However the Tyneside Passenger Transport Authority's review of the area's transport needs recognised that much of the route was worth electrifying within the Metro system, first

to Kenton Bank Foot, and perhaps eventually to the Airport. These plans reached fruition on 10 May 1981, when services were resumed between South Gosforth and Bank Foot. Intermediate stations were at Regent Centre, Wansbeck Road, and Fawdon. On 15 September 1985 the PTE opened a further station at Kingston Park. By special agreement, a limited number of goods services shared the Metro line, to Rowntrees sidings near Kingston Park (until 28 July 1988) and Prestwick Siding (until 6 March 1989). To allow clearance for the goods trains, the overhead wires on the branch were at 13ft 7in rather than the standard 12ft 1in.

Beyond Bank Foot the logical extension to Newcastle Airport took place on 17 November 1991, with an intermediate park and ride station at Callerton.

The Stations: West Gosforth
This two platform station was immediately west of the Great North Road. On the down platform was a collection of timber buildings, including the standard design of station building found at intermediate stations on this branch. Between 1900 and 1914 the NER was fond of equipping new or rebuilt stations with attractive timber buildings, one of which we have already encountered on the Coast Circle at Walker Gate, dating from 1908. At West Gosforth the building was single-storeyed under a pitched roof, containing a booking hall, general waiting room, and ladies' room. In front was an enclosed, glazed veranda with a small gable over the door. The station was electrically lit, but the lamp-posts also carried oil casement lamps. The nameboards were standard NER enamel type, with white letters on a reddish-brown background and white surround.

West Gosforth closed to passengers on 17 June 1929 and to all traffic on 14 August 1967.

Regent Centre
On 10 May 1981 a new Metro station opened on the site of West Gosforth. It takes its name from a nearby office development, in turn named after the adjacent, long-closed, Regent Pit. The new station is a major road/rail interchange similar to Four Lane Ends, with the two platforms beneath the entrance buildings.

Wansbeck Road
A two-platform Metro station was opened on 10 May 1981 on a new site, where the line crosses over Wansbeck Road. The slightly staggered platforms have standard Metro shelters, tall lamps, and yellow nameboards.

Coxlodge
The architect's plans of 1903 indicate that this station was expected to be called Fawdon. It opened on 1 June 1905. The main timber building on the down platform was of the standard line style. The up platform waiting shed was also of timber, with a glazed front. A low, brick-built signal box stood at the eastern end of the down platform, close to the level crossing. Coxlodge closed to passengers on 17

West Gosforth looking towards Newcastle. This is now the site of Regent Centre Metro Station. *(Lens of Sutton)*

Kenton Bank in 1959. This is the site of the present Bankfoot Station. *(Stations UK)*

Bankfoot was a single platform terminus from opening of the Metro until extension to the Airport. *(Alan Young)*

Callerton Parkway looking towards Newcastle in May 1998. Just beyond the platforms, the line drops at 1 in 33 to reach the level of the original Ponteland branch.

(Martin Bairstow)

June 1929. By 1959 the main building remained in a truncated form. Goods traffic, which in 1913 consisted of roadstone, continued until 6 December 1965. By 1973 the buildings and down platform had been removed. The signal box remained but has since been demolished.

In 1911 Coxlodge booked the fewest tickets of any station on the branch.

Fawdon
This Metro station opened on the site of Coxlodge on 10 May 1981. The platforms are staggered either side of the level crossing, the up platform being some yards to the west of the crossing. Standard Metro buildings and furniture are provided.

Kingston Park
This station, opened on 15 September 1985, was a late addition, funded by an underspend on the Metro construction project. It has two platforms and simple buildings.

Kenton Bank
This station opened on 1 June 1905 as Kenton, serving a local population of approximately 600. On 1 July 1923, under LNER ownership, it was renamed Kenton Bank to avoid confusion with the LNER station on the Mid-Suffolk Light Railway. There was a single platform, with standard timber building, a passing loop, and a signal box at the level crossing. Passenger services were withdrawn on 17 June 1929. Both the station building and the signal box were still standing 30 years after passenger closure.

Goods services ceased on 3 January 1966.

Bank Foot
When part of the branch re-opened on 10 May 1981, this was the single platform terminus. It is on the site of Kenton Bank station and has standard Metro buildings and fittings. A second platform was added when the Airport extension opened.

Callerton
The original Callerton station served a dispersed rural community with only some 800 people. It opened on 1 June 1905 and received the standard single-storey timber buildings. Although the railway widened to three tracks through the station, there was only a single platform. On 21 March 1915 the station buildings were destroyed by fire, but were rebuilt in the former style. A low, timber signal box stood between the platform and the level crossing. Passenger services were withdrawn on 17 June 1929. In 1963 the main building was still standing, together with a wooden shed.

Goods traffic in 1913, made up of potatoes, hay/clover, and livestock, reflected the rural surroundings of the station. Goods services ceased on 6 December 1965.

Callerton Parkway
Situated immediately to the south of the original station, this one opened on 17 November 1991 when the Metro was extended to Newcastle Airport. There is a large car park east of the platforms. The station serves as a rail-head for local hamlets, Ponteland,

Darras Hall, and more distant settlements towards Otterburn. Passenger accommodation is limited and of a different design from the 1981 stations. A feature of particular interest is the striking changes of gradient directly to the south east of the station.

Airport

The new terminus opened on 17 November 1991. It consists of an island platform with awning, giving direct access via a covered ramp to the airport entrance. The sunken site has made the station liable to flooding.

Ponteland

This had a single platform on the up side with a longer version of the single-storey timber building found at the intermediate stations. A glazed veranda extended for about two-thirds of the length and was decorated with two gables. A low timber signal box stood at the south east end of the platform. Several sidings were provided, one of which served a short goods platform. This was the busiest station on the branch, booking 32,084 tickets in 1911. Goods services continued until 14 August 1967.

The station building survived into the 1960s. Today there is no trace of the station, the site being occupied by a supermarket.

Darras Hall

Although two tracks passed through the station, there was only a single, timber platform on the up side. The building, like those of the Ponteland branch, was of timber, but the design was more elaborate to satisfy the exacting standards of the discerning local residents. The single-storey main building had twin pavilions; their gable-ends, together with the main gables, were decorated with a Tudoresque 'half-timber' design. Between the pavilions was a lean-to awning, front-supported by six pillars. There was also a second timber building on the platform. Long after closure, the station building was used by a church, but was eventually demolished in 1992/93.

Callerton viewed from a passing special in 1963.
(Stations UK)

Darras Hall station in use as a church hall in April 1977.
(Alan Young)

The Quayside Branch

Since Medieval times trade on the River Tyne had been vital to Newcastle. The deep, tidal water was navigable, but the steep river banks made movement of goods to and from the Quayside difficult.

Railway access to the river in Newcastle was provided by the ¾ mile single-track Quayside Branch, authorised on 28 July 1863, and opened on 1 June 1870. It was a goods line only throughout its life. It climbed from the Quayside to Manors in a semi-circle, largely in tunnel and cutting, at the remarkably steep gradient of 1 in 27. Steam locomotives hauled the trains until electrification on 5 June 1905.

In steam days the Quayside run was not a favourite job for footplatemen. Struggling up the gradient in a narrow tunnel, the driver and fireman contended with clouds of smoke and steam. When westerly winds blew, conditions were worse still as both ends of the tunnel faced west, and smoke could not escape. In wet weather the rails became slippery. Sometimes the driver had to ask his fireman to drag his shovel against the tunnel wall to discover if his engine was making progress up the hill!

K. Hoole's book *The Electric Locomotives of the North Eastern Railway* describes in detail the two Bo-Bo engines which worked the line throughout its electrified life. They were constructed by British Thomson-Houston (suppliers of the electrical equipment for the 1904 Coast passenger stock) and could haul six goods trains per hour from Quayside in 4½ minutes as well as performing general shunting duties. The locomotives could set off with a 150 ton train and haul it at 9-10 mph. under all weather conditions.

The tunnel was equipped with a third live rail (extending 20ft beyond the portals), and the open sections and yards had overhead wires. The locomotives carried a bow current-collector on one of the end bonnets (soon replaced by a cab-roof pantograph) for outdoor work, and current-collecting shoes on the bogies for the tunnel section. The engineman had to remember to retract the pantograph, using a rod through the cab roof, when entering the tunnel. The tunnel portals carried scars as evidence of some drivers' loss of concentration! The locomotives were also fitted with sandboxes at each end, aiding adhesion on the steep gradient. Trains were hauled, never propelled, on the branch.

After giving some 60 years' service the two locomotives were retired. Diesels took over on 29 February 1964 until closure on 16 June 1969. The demise of the branch reflected declining river traffic in central Newcastle.

One of the electric locomotives (26501) was scrapped. The other (26500) is preserved in the National Railway Museum at York.

Electric loco No. 1 (later No. 26500) on the Quayside in May 1920. Withdrawn in 1964, it is preserved at the National Railway Museum in York.   *(LCGB – Ken Nunn Collection)*

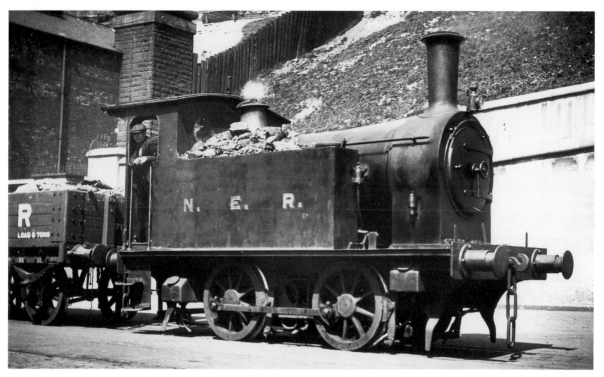

Class Y7 0-4-0T No. 519 on the Quayside in May 1920. Sister engine No.1310 is preserved on the Middleton Railway, Leeds.   *(LCGB – Ken Nunn Collection)*

26500 at Trafalgar Yard on a misty 29 February 1964, the final day of electric traction on the Quayside branch.   *(Ian S. Carr)*

The South Shields Branch

One of the 1955 Eastleigh built electric units at Pelaw with a South Shields to Newcastle working on 27 December 1962.   *(Ian S. Carr)*

The Route

The first 3³/₄ miles of the South Shields journey was shared with the Sunderland route. On our 1961 journey, we board a 1955 Eastleigh-built electric multiple unit at platform 6 in Newcastle Central. Negotiating the diamond crossing, our train passes the Castle Keep before crossing the High Level Bridge, allowing a magnificent view of the River Tyne. We are scarcely off the bridge when we reach **Gateshead (East)** (¹/₂ mile from Newcastle) announced by a black wooden nameboard. To our right Gateshead (West) platforms curve away sharply. Gateshead (East) is on a tight curve, and the trainshed is dark and uninviting. We remain above street level, and the tracks from King Edward Bridge and Gateshead Depot meet ours on the right at a trailing junction. After a straight stretch of under 100 yd the line curves sharply right, and there begins a stretch of almost a mile past the sidings of Borough Gardens Locomotive Shed.

Four tracks pass Felling and Pelaw, the southerly pair for passenger trains and two goods lines to our left. Beyond the sidings, **Felling** (2¹/₄ miles) is entered, with a large island platform serving the passenger lines. A long stretch in a cutting takes us

to **Pelaw** (3¹/₂ miles), also an island platform. Just beyond the station we cross the mineral line which opened as the Pelaw Main waggonway from near Chester-le-Street to the Tyne. Our route divides three ways close to the modern Pelaw Junction signal box. Two tracks to Washington curve away to our right. This is an important goods route, but its passenger service is negligible. The Sunderland line continues ahead, whilst we curve left on a route following the south bank of the Tyne, but we are usually over 500 yd from the river. A mile of open land, some farmed, some neglected, brings us into **Hebburn** (5¹/₂ miles), with factories, sidings, and terraced housing preceding the station. Housing and industry line the route to Jarrow. Shortly before Jarrow station, the former Pontop & Jarrow Railway is crossed, at a point where it splays into sidings serving a foundry.

Jarrow (6³/₄ miles) is dingy, without evidence of modernisation. Half-a-mile on we temporarily leave the built-up area. Crossing the River Don we look left across the fields to Jarrow Priory, and the large tidal pool of Jarrow Slake. Continuing towards Tyne Dock, to our right is pleasant farmland, though a housing estate at Simonside is encroaching upon it, and a trading estate has recently been built on our left. Sidings serving Tyne Dock leave at St. Bede's Junction and, crossing under Newcastle Road, a cutting begins. We slow down to approach a sharply left-curving covered way beneath the mineral line and sidings which carry the Tyne Dock-Consett iron ore trains. The passenger line from Sunderland trails in on our right. The original South Shields route leaves us on the same side, then we enter the island platform of **Tyne Dock** (9 miles), little changed since the days of the North Eastern Railway.

The winding route to High Shields is above street level, amongst terrace houses. Beyond **High Shields** (10¼ miles), terraces give way to a disorganised landscape of wasteland, factories, and sidings. The old Pontop & South Shields route joins from the right, and we enter the terminus at **South Shields** (11 miles). This is our journey's end, but sidings continue to the bank of the Tyne.

The Stations

The stations between Newcastle and South Shields were varied in character. All were Victorian, most buildings dating from between 1872 and 1896. They included island platforms at Felling, Pelaw, and Tyne

Dock, and side-platforms elsewhere. The platforms at Hebburn, Jarrow, Tyne Dock and High Shields were extended when the line was electrified. The Victorian buildings survived at every station until early 1972 when they were demolished and replaced with small, brick huts. Only South Shields kept its old buildings during this 'blitz'; this was the only station on the branch to remain staffed after 5 October 1969.

Whereas the Coast Circle stations were almost all electrically lit and re-signed by the LNER, then fitted with B.R. N.E Region nameboards, modernisation of South Shields stations seemed grudging and patchy. Throughout the 1960s gas lighting remained at Felling, Hebburn, Jarrow, Tyne Dock, High Shields, and South Shields. Vitreous enamel nameboards and totems were installed at Felling, Pelaw, Hebburn, High Shields, also at South Shields, where almost-unique double-sided totems were to be seen. In 1972 tall electric lamps appeared. Black and white 'corporate identity' nameplates were soon in place at each station.

Starting in 1979, all the South Shields branch stations were closed, either temporarily or permanently, for Metro works.

A dmu from Newcastle calls at Gateshead East on its way either to South Shields or Sunderland on 22 January 1965.   *(Kevin Hudspith)*

Gateshead (East)

Gateshead (East) station opened on 18 June 1844. It stood above the neighbouring streets, being immediately south of the High Level Bridge, which came into use in 1849. The two timber platforms were curved, and (from 1868) the northern end of the up platform met the end of Gateshead (West) down platform. Passengers entered from Wellington Street ('up' side), passed under both tracks, then climbed the stairs to the booking office and waiting rooms on the down platform. The approach to this platform was lit by a large semicircular window, and passenger entry to the platform was controlled by elegant iron railings. The upper storey of the buildings had 'school-board' windows, with matching door openings. A trainshed of curved cross-section covered the platforms, supported by plain girders, with a gap in the roof above the tracks. South of the trainshed a ridged awning covered the up platform, which extended many yards beyond the down platform. At the north end the down platform extended further, the up platform being curtailed by the junction of the line through Gateshead (West).

Into the early 1960s, Gateshead (East) retained LNER nameboards. Lighting was by electric bulbs in brick-shaped diffusers carrying the station name, of the style found at Manors (East). Signs simply read 'Gateshead'. Vitreous enamel nameboards were installed in about 1962.

On 5 October 1969 Gateshead (East) became unstaffed. By 1972 the station had changed dramatically. The trainshed and awning had been dismantled, and the remaining buildings on the down platform had their windows filled in. Previously the station seemed dark and dirty; now it was bleak and equally uninviting. As a concession to passenger comfort a shelter had been added on the down side. Tall electric lamps had been installed. From 1 May 1972 it was acknowledged that there was no longer a Gateshead (West), so East was dropped from the name.

The station was inconveniently sited. Being adjacent to the river there was no catchment to the north, and it was not close enough to Gateshead's shopping centre to be useful. The climb to the platforms might also have deterred potential passengers. With the opening of the more central Metro station, this one closed a week later, on 23 November 1981. The former East station remained intact until the early 1990s when it was demolished almost without trace: a challenging task considering its position on bridges above road level.

Gateshead (West)

The two platforms opened on 1 December 1868. They curved sharply away from the East station, and had a tall, massively-gabled main building on the south platform, and a ridged trainshed. There was a glazed screen at each end of the south platform. The north building was merely a supporting wall for the

Gateshead West, 10 October 1965, seen from the footbridge leading to the East Station (on the extreme left). Closure is only three weeks away when the single weekday and two Saturday trains will cease to call.   *(Kevin Hudspith)*

A Newcastle bound dmu passes Felling on a misty 12 February 1972. Demolition of the awnings is at an advanced stage.   *(Trevor Ermel)*

trainshed. Gas lighting, fixed to telegraph poles on the open platforms, gave way to electricity in LNER times. The trainshed survived into the 1960s, but by 1962 its roofing remained only over the south platform.

The service at Gateshead (West) in *Bradshaw* of April 1910 was varied and frequent, with trains to and from Durham, Consett, and Dunston-on-Tyne. By July 1938 the Dunston service had ceased, but trains on the other routes still regularly called at Gateshead. However, in the first British Railways timetable (May 1948), Consett trains no longer called, and the only departures were at 5.55a.m. to Darlington via Bishop Auckland and 6.1a.m. to Durham. In the reverse direction only the 8.34a.m. ex-Darlington and the 8.48a.m. ex-Durham called at Gateshead (West). By contrast, East had some 160 departures.

In its final appearance in the public timetable of September 1965, Gateshead (West) was relegated to the footnotes, with the paltry service of an 08.34 (weekdays) and 14.28 (Saturdays only), both ex-Darlington, and no trains in the opposite direction. Gateshead (West) quietly passed away on 1 November 1965, but its platforms remain.

Gateshed Greenesfield

This station was open from 15 January 1839 until 30 August 1850, when traffic was diverted across the High Level Bridge to Newcastle. It was designed by G. T. Andrews, the architect of Richmond, Pocklington, Whitby Town and other fine stations in the North East. There was an overall roof behind a classical facade, with pilastered pavilions flanking a central colonnaded portico and a deeply corniced parapet. The offices were within a house at one end of the station. Although the station has disappeared, the adjacent Greenesfield Hotel, listed Grade II, survives as railway offices.

Gateshead Metro

On 15 November 1981 this underground station opened, with the system's largest bus interchange facilities. From a concourse area with the Northern Travelcard Centre at ground level, there is stair and escalator access to a ticketing area, and lift and escalator access to the platform. The site is convenient for central Gateshead, consequently it is heavily used.

Gateshead Stadium

Known at the planning stage as Old Fold, this station opened on 15 November 1981. There is an island platform with simple buildings, approached by a ramp.

Felling

The first station, on the Brandling Junction Railway, opened on 5 September 1839. It closed on 18 November 1896, to be replaced by a new one a little to the west. The main building was of stone and extremely small. Tall lancet windows filled a gabled projection. Immediately south east was a separate building containing a waiting room, with a pitched roof carried forward as an awning, supported by solid side brackets. A large villa with a first floor bay window on the railway side completed the ensemble. Despite periods of neglect, the small main building is still standing.

Felling (second station)

Opened on 18 November 1896 this possessed a wide island platform serving the southern pair of tracks. Its unremarkable brick buildings were dwarfed by a huge, ridged awning with generous glazed end-screens, through which chimneys from the station offices and waiting rooms projected. The platform was approached by a ramp down from the small, brick entrance building on Sunderland Road, enclosed by stepped timber sections under curved roofs.

Until the late 1950s the station was well-tended, with lawns and flowerbeds west of the buildings. It remained gas-lit, and B.R. totems and nameboards were installed. Goods services ceased on 2 August 1965. From 5 October 1969 Felling was unstaffed, and the buildings were soon vandalised. The nameboards were made illegible by graffiti. All buildings and platform furniture, including the covering ramp, were swept away in February 1972, to be replaced by a tiny shelter and tall electric lamps. This station closed on 5 November 1979 and has given way to the Metro station on the same site.

Winter Sunday services were withdrawn from Felling by the 1961-62 timetable.

Heworth

This new station opened on 5 November 1979, when Felling and Pelaw closed. B.R. services at the northern pair of platforms were joined by Metro trains at the two southern platforms on 15 November 1981 – their temporary terminus until the South Shields route was re-opened.

Pelaw Junction (First and second stations)

The first station at Pelaw opened on 5 September 1839 but was closed by 1857, and replaced by another, 180yd to the east. The second station lasted until 18 November 1896, when a further station was built on the original site.

Pelaw (Third station)

Known also as Pelaw Junction, this opened on 18 November 1896. Like Felling, it had one wide island platform. Its lengthy brick building was undistinguished. Flat awnings with deep wooden valances, ending with glazed screens fronted each platform face. A ramp with sloping timber sides, windows, and a curved roof led down to the platform, disappearing into a timber shed which clad the end of the platform building. The awning valance continued around this shed, adding a touch of decoration.

In about 1961 gas lighting was replaced by electric lamps on concrete posts in the then-fashionable style, to which totems were fixed. Goods services ended on 4 October 1965.

Pelaw underwent the same changes as Felling from unstaffing on 5 October 1969, through reconstruction in 1972, to closure on 5 November 1979. The station was demolished, and at the time there was no intention to replace it.

Pelaw (Fourth station)

A decision was taken by the Metro to re-instate Pelaw and use it instead of Heworth as a terminus for some services. Accordingly a new island platform station was opened on 16 September 1985, some 18 months after the Metro had opened through Pelaw.

Hebburn

On 1 March 1872 Hebburn opened on the new NER line from Pelaw to Tyne Dock. There were two platforms, with the main buildings on the up side. A plain L-shaped villa was flanked to the north by a brick flat-roofed single storey building with an immense chimney stack, housing the gentlemen's toilet. At its other side, a single storey extension ended with a pavilion, from which a square bay window projected under a tiny pitched roof. This style in single-storey twin-pavilion form was found at Lintz Green and some other 1860s Scotswood-Blackhill stations. North of the other buildings, a timber shed with a pitched roof and windows served as a waiting room. A further timber shed stood beside the iron lattice footbridge which flanked the stone bridge carrying Station Road across the line at the south end of the platforms. The down platform had a single storey pitched-roofed building with glazed front containing a waiting room.

Hebburn remained gas-lit, and even in the late 1960s had some post-mounted casement laps, when most NE Region gas-lit stations had moved onto the hanging Sugg-style. In about 1962 NE Region totems and nameboards were installed.

Unstaffed from 5 October 1969, Hebburn received the same treatment as its neighbouring stations, and by March 1972 the buildings had gone, leaving only nameboards and some gas lamps. New shelters and electric lighting were added. The station closed on 1 June 1981 for Metro work. The Metro station, opened on 24 March 1984, has staggered platforms and simple buildings. The up platform is on the original site, whilst the other is beyond Station Road.

Jarrow

This station opened on 1 March 1872. The main building on the down platform was brick-built and two-storeyed with gables facing the platform, and between them a lean-to shelter. The opposite platform also had a long, lean-to shelter. Later (c.1895-1905) a cross between a trainshed and awnings was installed, with the older shelters retained. On each platform centrally placed columns with ornate spandrels supported the long, ridged awnings roofed with glass, but at frequent intervals girders spanned the tracks. The awnings had delicate ironwork valances, but these were removed by 1960. A footbridge connected the platforms. A signal box stood beneath the up platform awning.

Jarrow station has been an important source of traffic, but was particularly so before 1920 when the town's shipyards were busy.

Whilst minor attempts at modernisation had been made at some other stations on the line, by the

A train of 1937 stock leaving Pelaw for South Shields about 1946. This stock was usually confined to the north side of the River.
(W. Hubert Foster, courtesy John Holroyd)

Passengers and parcels await a Newcastle dmu at Hebburn in 1966. *(Gordon Biddle)*

Jarrow looking towards Hebburn in 1959. The original lean-to awning can be seen on the extreme right beneath the later ridged awning.
(Stations UK)

late 1960s Jarrow seemed stuck in a time-warp. The dirty awnings admitted little daylight, and the platforms were dimly lit by gas. Two faded, wooden nameboards were the only evidence of the station name. It was unstaffed from 5 October 1969, and the work begun by vandals was completed by British Rail in early 1972. By March the awnings and main buildings had gone, but the original shelter on the down platform survived briefly. The old nameboards remained, and temporary gas lamps had been rigged up on posts to replace those which had hung from the awning. New shelters were under construction, and electric lighting soon followed. Nine years later it all changed again when Jarrow closed on 1 June 1981 for Metro work, to re-open on 24 March 1984. Standard Metro buildings are on both platforms. The up side is also graced by a steel sculpture depicting the 1934 Jarrow March.

Bede

This new station, opened on 24 March 1984, serves Bede Trading Estate, which derives its name from the Venerable Bede, the eighth century historian, who resided at Jarrow Priory. The two staggered platforms have standard Metro buildings

Tyne Dock

There was a station on this site from 19 June 1839 on the Brandling Junction Railway. A new one was authorised on 10 February 1881. Built with a wide island platform, the single-storey building resembled those at Felling and Pelaw. A broad, hipped awning surrounded the building, supported by slender columns with bulbous bases.

There was no modernisation until early 1972,

when everything on the platform was demolished. For the previous decade, one LNER wooden nameboard at the north end, aided by ancient strips of paper on some windows, announced the station's name, and lighting was by gas.

It closed on 1 June 1981, to be replaced by a Metro station on an adjacent site. The features of the new site have called for more substantial buildings than at some other Metro stations.

High Shields (First station)

The original Brandling Junction Railway station was open from 19 June 1839 until 2 June 1879, when the NER replaced it with a new one 200yd to the north.

High Shields (Second station)

Situated on a reverse-curve above street level, High Shields opened on 2 June 1879. The main building on the up platform had some pretence to elegance, entered through a porte-cochere, which G. Biddle dismisses as clumsy, apologetic, and looking like an afterthought. At platform level the building was unremarkable, dominated by a large, ridged awning, and supported towards its front by ten narrow columns. These carried elaborate iron spandrels with a floral motif. The down platform had a modest waiting shelter.

High Shields was gas-lit until 1972, N.E. Region nameboards and totems were added in about 1962. Once again, unstaffing on 5 October 1969 was followed by the demolition of all platform buildings in early 1972. The station closed on 1 June 1981 and has not re-opened because the Metro has been diverted via Chichester.

At High Shields, the main buildings were graced by a generously sized awning.   (Gordon Biddle)

A class 101 is about to leave South Shields for Newcastle on 5 January 1973. *(Alan Young)*

Chichester
The Metro between Tyne Dock and South Shields (Garden Lane Junction) closely follows the Stanhope & Tyne route of 1834. Chichester is on this section and opened with the line on 24 March 1984. It is a bus/rail interchange point.

South Shields (First station)
This was opened by the Pontop & South Shields Railway on 16 April 1835. It closed on 19 August 1844 when trains were diverted to the Third South Shields station.

South Shields (Second station)
The Brandling Junction Railway opened its terminus on 19 June 1839. A contemporary sketch shows that the building was a single storey, hipped-roof structure. On 17 December 1842 it closed when the line was extended to Market Place.

South Shields (Third station)
Opened by the Brandling Junction Railway, this station replaced their earlier one on 17 December 1842. It survived until 2 June 1879, giving way to the fourth station.

South Shields (Fourth station)
This station opened on 2 June 1879. It proved more durable than its predecessors, handling passenger traffic until 1 June 1981.

There were two platforms, built on a pronounced curve, with three tracks between them. Beyond, the line continued to the old Stanhope & Tyne staiths. The brick building on the up platform was plain and very similar to that at Cullercoats, which was built three years later. The frontage was unremarkable, with segmental-headed openings, but at South Shields a rose window repeated on the platform side, even though it only overlooked the slope of the overall roof. This was pitched in one broad span, and was probably the work of William Peachey, NER architect 1876-77. The curving site lent perspective to the roof, relieving its plainness. The platforms were connected by an iron latticework footbridge.

Whilst the intermediate stations were all unstaffed in 1969 and, soon after, 'simplified', South Shields survived intact and received modernised lighting and signing. Permanent closure came on 1 June 1981. The Metro terminates about 100yd south at a fifth station! The fourth was relieved of its trainshed, down platform and backwall, but the main building and up platform remained in a truncated form as a walkway to the new station for Metro staff. However, demolition of the building was advanced in summer 1998.

South Shields (Fifth station)
This new single platform Metro terminus was opened on 24 March 1984. It is conveniently situated above King Street, the main shopping thoroughfare.

Tickets Issued

	1911	1951	1967
Gateshead *(combined)*	491,920	134,246	68,629
Felling	284,026	147,241	62,526
Pelaw	207,536	58,340	74,847
Hebburn	415,656	197,130	149,029
Jarrow	625,200	263,977	126,026
Tyne Dock	384,137	364,088	168,278
High Shields	301,687	182,052	44,483
South Shields	649,785	318,459	262,867

The South Shields, Marsden and Whitburn Colliery Railway

0-6-0 No. 6 of the South Shields, Marsden & Whitburn Colliery Railway was a former NER '398' class designed by Edward Fletcher in the 1870s. It is seen near Marsden in June 1913.
(LCGB – Ken Nunn Collection)

Local people knew this line and its train as 'The Rattler'. It was a fascinating railway, and no apology is made for including it as a Tyneside suburban line.

The railway was unusual in being detached from any other passenger line. It was shortest railway to appear in *Bradshaw*, yet had the longest name. Though it survived into the British Railways era, the North Eastern Region timetable omitted it. Being owned by a coal company, it was nationalised when the National Coal Board was established in 1947. Its southern terminus in later years was not where the timetable or Ordnance Survey maps indicated. The line even possessed an unadvertised station whose popular and official names differed!

Because the railway was purely to serve a colliery it opened without plans having to go before Parliament. Only in 1926 did the Ministry of Transport confer Light Railway status when part of its route was deviated. The line was opened in May 1879 by the Harton Coal Company, to serve its new Whitburn Colliery. The single-line route was 3¼ miles in length from South Shields (Westoe Lane) station to Whitburn Colliery miners' platform. The Harton company constructed a system of railways connecting the Stanhope & Tyne (formerly Pontop & South Shields) line to the SSM&WCR at South Shields (Westoe Lane) station. From Westoe Lane the SSM&WCR travelled east for 500yd, where it veered south east and ran close to the coast for the rest of its route. About 1½ miles from Westoe Lane was Marsden Cottage Halt, which opened in about 1900, but was absent from public timetables. One mile further on was the southern terminus for the public at Marsden station. Miners travelled another half-mile to Whitburn Colliery. The journey from Westoe Lane to Marsden took ten minutes.

From its opening to coal traffic, miners were also conveyed. Members of the public were carried from March 1885, but because the railway had opened without an Act of Parliament, carriage of fare-paying passengers was illegal, and they had to sign a disclaimer before travelling. To satisfy the Board of Trade, the 'informal' public service was discontinued. Official passenger trains began on 19 March 1888 between South Shields (Westoe Lane) and Marsden, half a mile north of the miners' platform at Whitburn, once the line had been improved and signals installed to the Board of Trade's satisfaction. The public's interest in this railway was due to the closeness of Marsden station to the bay, with its grotto, sands, and (until it collapsed in 1996!) spectacular natural arch. The popularity of this destination was reflected in summer 1890 by Sunday trains outnumbering weekday trains.

In the mid-1920s it was necessary to deviate the railway for ¾ mile to make way for a new coastal road, and the line was shifted about 50yd inland. Marsden station was on the abandoned stretch, but it was not replaced. Instead passengers travelled the short extra distance to Whitburn miners' platform. After the deviation opened in 1929, *Bradshaw* continued to call the southern terminus Marsden. Even more confusing for the historian, the 1953 Ordnance Survey One-inch map showed Marsden station as open on its pre-1929 site, with none at Whitburn Colliery!

The station at Westoe Lane had one platform and a very large, brick building, with three projecting blocks, embellished by curved gables above central dormers, and two simple lean-to awnings between the blocks. Shortly before closure, a visitor remarked on the absence of nameboards, other signs, advertisements, seats, and porters. A nameboard was provided at an earlier date. Marsden Cottage Halt, on the coast side of the line, had a random-stone platform. In the late 1930s a simple brick shelter and a nameboard (without 'Halt') were provided, but by the 1950s corrugated iron shelters had appeared either side of the brick shelter, and the nameboard had gone. Locally this halt was known as Salmon's Hall. The original Marsden station had an imitation stone, faintly Tudor building. Whitburn Colliery had a narrow platform east of the track with electric lighting, and no buildings other than a ticket office at its southern end.

The passenger service in *Bradshaw* of July 1938 shows some sixteen weekday and eight Sunday trains in each direction. Timings suited the miners' needs: thus the strangely timed 3.55, 4.30, and 5.30a.m. weekday departures from Westoe Lane. The final tables before closure showed a Monday to Friday only service of twelve trains each way.

The SSM&WCR remained the property of the Harton company until the NCB was created on 1 January 1947. For motive power the railway used the cast-off locomotives from other companies, mostly ex-NER; one locomotive of 1856, rebuilt in 1881, was used on the line until about 1950! In 1953, eight locomotives were used on the line. Saddle tanks and ex-NER 0-6-0s drew four- and six-wheeled coaches formerly belonging to the Great Eastern and Great North of Scotland Railways, some dating from the 1890s. The GNSR coaches apparently came south to County Durham for the Stockton & Darlington centenary celebrations, never to return to Scotland! The normal arrangement for passenger haulage was that one engine worked the line for a week at a time.

At Westoe Lane the SSM&WCR met the Harton company's network of some 4½ miles. This was operated by overhead 500v DC traction, installed in 1908.

Passenger traffic on the SSM&WCR was subject to bus competition on the nearby coast road, yet the service continued until 20 November 1953. Whitburn Colliery closed on 8 June 1968. The line remained in place for some months, and was used by a railtour on 7 September 1968. The rails were removed by July 1969 as far as Mowbray Road in South Shields, and the trackbed can now be followed beside the coastal road past Marsden.

Westoe Lane station site is occupied by houses and gardens, but the trackbed to the east was still undeveloped in summer 1998.

No. 10, also an ex NER '398' class, in charge of the 3.15pm Whitburn to South Shields on 8 May 1923.
(LCGB – Ken Nunn Collection)

Patrons on the 7 September 1968 railtour enjoy a bracing trip along the Coast towards Whitburn. By this time, the railway had no passenger stock.
(Martin Bairstow Collection)

The Tyne & Wear Metro

The Metro was diverted away from the old railway alignment in order to reach this new Byker Station. A Coast to St James train calls in April 1988. *(Martin Bairstow)*

The need for the Metro

The Tyne and Wear area experienced a steady increase in road traffic through the 1960s. The region's geography created particular problems. The limited number of river crossing points, most of them close to the hearts of Newcastle and Gateshead, caused difficulties for road transport converging on these centres. The A1 road passed through the centres of Newcastle and Gateshead. The west of Newcastle and Gateshead was poorly served by rail: the Newcastle-Carlisle line, being so close to the Tyne, had a limited catchment area for its stations at Elswick and Scotswood, which closed in 1967. Railways did not penetrate the main shopping and commercial centre of Newcastle, with Newcastle Central too far south and Manors too far east.

Developments in the 1960s made the situation worse. The local railways suffered dis-investment, as the electric infrastructure was removed. A new central motorway system, involving the destruction of many buildings, was planned to relieve pressure on the road system. Only fragments of the proposed new inner road system were actually constructed at that time.

Late in the 1960s a partnership of central and local government and transport operators drew up the Tyne Wear Plan. This identified the region's transport problems and recommended significant investment in public transport on segregated routes, based on the existing railway system. Lines and stations would require upgrading, and the central area would require improved access.

On 1 April 1969 the Tyneside Passenger Transport Authority was formed. Various options for transport improvements were considered by their consultants. The existing railway system was inadequate for the region's needs, and any attempts to economise by reducing services would make trains even less attractive. One proposal was to remove the rail tracks and use their routes as dedicated busways reached by ramps from the road system. However buses would be slowed down by the congestion of city centre roads to which they were contributing. On busways they would be limited to 40mph by the width of the old railway formation, unless immense sums were spent on widening embankments, bridges, and cuttings. Moreover British Rail would continue operating on some routes.

Another proposal was to rely entirely on buses using ordinary roads. However this would delay them, add to congestion, and be expensive in manpower, even if initial investment costs were low.

Finally, a rapid light transit rail system could be used, incorporating some of the existing rail routes, extending them into the city centre, and connecting with buses serving areas without railways. One-man-operated electric railcars (or trams) with high acceleration would provide the service. This is the proposal which was adopted.

The Tyneside Metropolitan Railway Act 1973 was passed, contracts were let, and construction began. Tyne & Wear County (established on 1 April 1974) supported the project. Seventy years after its pioneering work in upgrading the suburban railways, Tyneside was again breaking new ground. The Metro was far more than just a new railway: it was the first comprehensive approach to transport provision in any British city. Care was taken to enable all sectors of society to travel easily within Tyneside, and resources were not squandered in helping some people to the disadvantage of others.

The Metro route

The essence of the Metro has been re-electrification of the Coast Circle from Jesmond via Tynemouth to Heaton Junction. The 'inner' sections of the Circle and South Shields routes have been replaced by new lines, largely underground, through the centres of Newcastle and Gateshead. The South Shields route is re-electrified from near Felling to South Shields, but diverted between Tyne Dock and South Shields.

Monument is the main interchange at the heart of Newcastle's shopping centre. The underground section serves Newcastle Central station, and a 'branch' serves St. James' Park football ground. Part of the Ponteland branch has re-opened, initially as far as Bank Foot.

In addition to four miles of tunnels under central Newcastle and Gateshead, the Tyne is crossed on the steel girder Queen Elizabeth Bridge 81ft above high tide water – sufficient to allow navigation – and 540ft long. The slender, curving concrete Byker Viaduct across the Ouseburn valley stands 98ft above the valley floor, stretches for 1/2 mile and has 18 spans, the longest being 226ft.

Rail/road interchanges are at Four Lane Ends, North Shields, Byker, Regent Centre, Chichester, Gateshead, Jarrow and Wallsend. A new rail/road interchange at Heworth is used by South Shields Metro and Sunderland rail services. The Metro Control Centre is at South Gosforth.

The Metro enjoys exclusive use of most of its route, but a special agreement was made with ICI (Callerton) and Rowntree (Coxlodge) allowing goods services to their sidings via Benton SW curve. These trains last ran to Callerton in 1989 and Coxlodge in 1987. Between Benton SE curve and Backworth Junction goods services linking the Bedlington line and the East Coast main line run on segregated track; and between Pelaw and Tyne Dock the Metro uses one line of the double track whilst goods trains use the other.

Most of the former BR stations have been retained. Jesmond, Heaton, and Tyne Dock stations were just off the Metro route: Jesmond and Tyne Dock were re-sited, and Heaton was replaced by

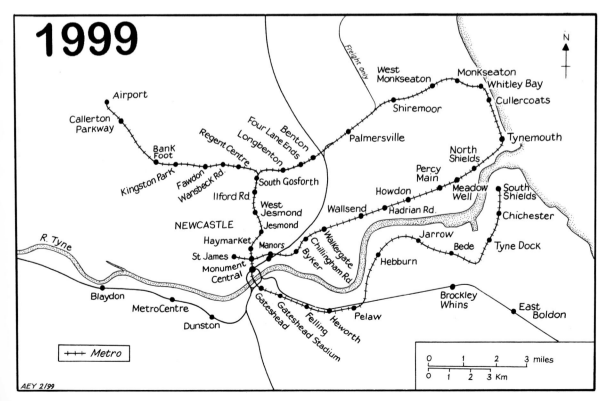

Chillingham Road and Byker. Backworth and Pelaw were closed with no immediate intention of replacement. Many new stations have opened and, most importantly, the Bank Foot branch was extended to the Airport in 1991.

Preparations for opening

National economic problems and trade unions disputes dogged the Metro project. At times abandonment seemed likely, with the prospect of half-completed tunnels being used for mushroom-growing! It became clear that its budget of £65m would be greatly exceeded; the final cost was £265m. Part of this over-run was due to the massive inflation of the 1970s. In preparation for Metro operation, local railway services were progressively withdrawn. As each section closed, 'Rail-Link' bus services were temporarily introduced.

The Metro adopted 1500 volt d.c. overhead electrification. The rolling stock consists of twin-articulated units carried on three bogies. Each two-section vehicle is 91ft 3in long and of lightweight construction. The units are designed for one-person operation. The car bodies rest on air suspension to provide a smooth ride, and resilient wheels and modern transmission ensure quietness. The twin-units can operate singly, or coupled in pairs, according to traffic needs. Each twin-unit has 84 seats, with space for 188 standing passengers. Four wide push-button operated doors are on each side, closed by the driver following a loud buzz and an invitation to 'stand clear of the doors'. Metro trains observe a speed limit of 50mph. The fleet of Metro cars, numbered 4003 to 4090, was constructed by Metro-Cammell.

Before Metro trains entered service, the public was welcome to inspect them on a test track at Middle Engine Lane. Prototype cars 4001 and 4002 were delivered in 1975. They underwent stringent trials and were used for crew training. These cars joined the fleet in 1987 after modification.

The Metro in action

The Metro system opened in stages. The first section opened on 11 August 1980 between Haymarket and Tynemouth via Benton. South Gosforth to Bank Foot followed on 10 May 1981. The Haymarket line was extended to Heworth on 15 November 1981, and Tynemouth to St. James was added on 14 November 1982, allowing interchange at Monument. From Heworth the Metro reached South Shields on 24 March 1984. Finally Bank Foot to Airport opened on 17 November 1991, increasing the system to 36.9 route-miles.

The Metro was designed to make trains and stations accessible to disabled people. Stations have ramp access, and the platform height conforms with the height of the car floors. Staff are kept to a minimum by using ticket machines which give the correct change. To deter fare-dodgers, roving teams of inspectors board trains at random. Closed-circuit television was installed from the outset allowing train and passenger movements to be monitored,

and a public address system was installed at stations to broadcast travel information. Amidst the high-tech features, the roller-blind train departure indicators seemed incongruous. These have now given way to electronic indicators, which also state when the next train is expected.

The Metro house style was chosen to complement Newcastle's buses. Metro cars were turned out in 'Newcastle cadmium yellow' for the lower panel, separated from the upper white panel by a French blue stripe. The roof was 'storm grey'. In 1980 cars bore the logos of the Passenger Transport Executive and of Tyne & Wear County Council. After the Metropolitan County Councils were abolished and buses were deregulated, the Metro's own identity was promoted with the big, black M, as used at stations. More recently a device incorporating the letters T and W has been adopted. Trains have also appeared in various special liveries during the 1990s, including an evocative 19th Century pastiche.

Metro stations are identified from the street by a post-mounted yellow cube bearing a large M. Nameboards are also yellow, originally with chocolate tubular surrounds. During the 1990s a variety of colour schemes was adopted when stations were repainted.

The Metro timetable changed as the network expanded. After 1984 when the South Shields line opened the service operated was:

Yellowline   Heworth-St. James via Benton and Tynemouth
Redline   Heworth-Benton
Greenline   South Shields-Bank Foot
Blueline   North Shields-St. James

In 1999 the service is:

Yellowline   Pelaw-St. James via Benton and Tynemouth
                  Pelaw-Benton (Saturdays only)
Greenline   South Shields-Airport

Trains run frequently enough to make it unnecessary to consult a timetable. On each line the weekday daytime service runs at ten-minute intervals, increased to seven/eight at peak times, and fifteen-minute intervals in evenings and all day Sunday. On Saturdays the Yellowline service is augmented by ten-minutely trains between Pelaw and Benton giving 18 trains an hour between Pelaw and South Gosforth.

Where next for the suburban railways?

The peak year of Metro patronage was 1985 with 59.1 million boardings. By 1997/98 boardings had declined by 40%. This was due to deregulation of buses in 1986 and consequent loss of rail/road public transport integration; increasing car ownership; greater dispersal of the region's population; increase of fares above the rate of inflation; and reductions in the availability of concessionary fares. Nevertheless the Metro is considered a success by both the Tyne & Wear Passenger Transport Authority, and its Executive *(Nexus)*. Extension of the system to Sunderland is

One of the attractions of the Metro trains, now lost on most other railways, is the forward view of the route ahead.
(Martin Bairstow)

The Tyne & Wear Metro is the only British railway still operating its own ferry – the half hourly service between North and South Shields. The 'Shieldsman' leaves North Shields on 3 May 1998.
(Martin Bairstow)

The last load to leave Rowntree's factory at Fawdon behind 31 173 on 30 January 1987. The demise of this traffic meant the end of freight on the Metro between here and Benton. *(N. E. Stead)*

planned. This 11½ mile Metro extension would share Railtrack metals to Sunderland station then follow the course of the former Durham line, terminating at South Hylton. The project is costed at £97m and should attract 8-11 million more passengers to the Metro. New stations are planned at Fellgate (between Pelaw and Brockley Whins); Roker and Monkwearmouth (between Seaburn and Sunderland); and Civic Centre, University, Millfield, and Pallion on the South Hylton section.

Further rail additions to the Metro appear unlikely, but 'Metro-complementary routes' – a term which avoids mention of any specific transport mode – have been identified. These would link such locations as Washington, Killingworth, Throckley, and MetroCentre to the system. Meanwhile, *Northern Spirit* is investigating possible restoration of passenger services between Backworth and Ashington and of local trains on the East Coast main line to serve Heaton, Forest Hall, Bensham, and Birtley.

Passenger boardings at Metro stations

	Annual 1995-6	% drop since	peak year
Monument	5,322,816	30	1986
Haymarket	3,091,328	33	1985
Gateshead	2,611,275	67	1985
Heworth	2,278,987	47	1985
Central Station	2,160,160	42	1984
North Shields	1,212,933	43	1988
South Shields	997,542	29	1985
West Jesmond	966,467	39	1985
Jesmond	915,787	35	1985
Wallsend	880,749	59	1985
South Gosforth	847,744	59	1985
Four Lane Ends	823,968	58	1984
Whitley Bay	819,276	35	1985
Regent Centre	745,028	37	1985
Jarrow	714,162	32	1985
Chichester	664,994	32	1985
Pelaw	616,868	29	1990
Hebburn	601,122	32	1984
Tynemouth	583,603	35	1985
Longbenton	549,295	43	1984
Monkseaton	542,777	38	1985
Felling	529,847	36	1984
Howdon	500,857	42	1985
Byker	498,406	51	1985
Cullercoats	474,735	43	1985
West Monkseaton	474,630	19	1985
Shiremoor	460,188	30	1985
Gateshead Stadium	441,000	48	1985
Tyne Dock	410,290	37	1985
Kingston Park	407,683	34	1987
Fawdon	378,328	38	1985
Walkergate	356,638	51	1985
Benton	348,243	43	1984
Percy Main	268,156	51	1987
Meadow Well	253,505	57	1987
Airport	251,263	17	1992
St. James	242,712	46	1985
Wansbeck Road	233,170	44	1985
Ilford Road	222,742	45	1985
Palmersville	222,481	26	1987
Chillingham Road	220,187	61	1985
Bede	215,495	39	1987
Manors	198,706	24	1991
Hadrian Road	170,967	53	1985
Bank Foot	158,610	68	1984
Callerton Parkway	59,440	40	1992

This table shows the decline in patronage described on page 92. By 1998, the fall appeared to have 'bottomed out'.

The clock tower at Whitley Bay is a North Eastern Railway feature which has survived into the Metro era.
(Martin Bairstow)

Appendices

NEWCASTLE - COAST CIRCLE VIA BENTON AND WALLSEND

Opened

20. 6.1839	Carliol Square - Shields 1st station (North Shields)
29. 3.1847	Shields - Tynemouth (Newcastle & Berwick terminus)
29. 8.1850	Manors - Newcastle Central
1. 4.1861	Whitley - Tynemouth (1st B&T station)
27. 6.1864	New Bridge Street - Whitley. Branch to Tynemouth (2nd B&T station)
1865	Tynemouth (2nd B&T) - Tynemouth (3rd B&T)
3. 7.1882	Monkseaton - North Shields coastal deviation
1. 5.1903	Benton SW curve
6.1904	Hartley - Monkseaton (Avenue Branch) reopened
1. 7.1904	Benton SE curve
1905	South Gosforth West Jn. - East Jn.
1. 1.1909	Manors Junction - New Bridge Street
9.10.1910	Deviation via new Whitley Bay station
25. 7.1915	Deviation via new Monkseaton station
1940	Benton NW curve (authorised 1902)

Closed

29. 8.1850	Branch to Carliol Square station
27. 6.1864	Holywell - Percy Main via Prospect Hill. Hartley - Whitley
3. 7.1882	Monkseaton - ex-B&T North Shields and Tynemouth termini (goods to first B&T station withdrawn on 1 May 1971)
3. 7.1882	Tynemouth (ex - N&B) branch. (closed to goods 2.3.1959)
1. 1.1909	Branch to New Bridge Street
9.10.1910	1882 route through Whitley Bay
25. 7.1915	1860 route through Monkseaton
4.12.1967	Branch to New Bridge Street Goods
3. 5.1976	Benton NW curve. (passengers; closed entirely on 8.1.1978)
23. 1.1978	Newcastle Central (Manors Jn) - West Monkseaton (via Benton)
23. 1.1978	Benton SE curve (passengers)
10. 9.1979	West Monkseaton - Tynemouth
11. 8.1980	Heaton Jn - Tynemouth

Metro openings and reopenings (M = Metro station on new route)

11. 8.1980	Haymarket - Tynemouth (via Benton)
15.11.1981	Haymarket - Heworth
14.11.1982	St James - Tynemouth

Stations	Opened	Closed (passengers)	Closed (goods)	Reopened (passengers)
Newcastle Central	29. 8.1850			
Central M	15.11.1981			
Haymarket M	11. 8.1980			
Manors North	1. 1.1909	23. 1.1978		
New Bridge Street	27. 6.1864	1. 1.1909	4.12.1967	
Jesmond	27. 6.1864	23. 1.1978		(re-sited)
Jesmond M	11. 8.1980			
West Jesmond	1.12.1900	23. 1.1978	14. 8.1967	11. 8.1980
Moor Edge	?	?		
Ilford Road	11. 8.1980			
South Gosforth	27. 6.1864	23. 1.1978	14. 8.1967	11. 8.1980
Longbenton	14. 7.1947	23. 1.1978		11. 8.1980
Long Benton	27. 6.1864	1. 3.1871		
Four Lane Ends	11. 8.1980			
Benton	1. 3.1871	23. 1.1978	14. 8.1967	11. 8.1980
Forest Hall	27. 6.1864	1. 3.1871		
Palmersville	19. 3.1986			
Benton Square	1. 7.1909	20. 9.1915		
Backworth	27. 6.1864	13. 6.1977		
Shiremoor	11. 8.1980			
West Monkseaton	2. 3.1933	10. 9.1979		11. 8.1980
Monkseaton	31.10.1860	25. 7.1915		(re-sited)
Monkseaton	25. 7.1915	10. 9.1979	2. 3.1959	11. 8.1980
Whitley Bay	3. 7.1882	9.10.1910		(re-sited)
Whitley Bay	9.10.1910	10. 9.1979		11. 8.1980
Cullercoats	27. 6.1864	7. 7.1882	7. 7.1882	(re-sited)
Cullercoats	7. 7.1882	10. 9.1979	10. 2.1964	11. 8.1980
N Shields Terminus	1. 4.1861	7. 7.1882	1. 5.1971	
N Shields Station	27. 6.1864	7. 7.1882		
Tynemouth	1865	7. 7.1882		
Tynemouth	29.3.1847	3. 7.1882	2. 3.1959	
Tynemouth	7. 7.1882		2. 3.1959	
North Shields	2. 6.1839		1890	
North Shields	1890	11. 8.1980	14.11.1982	
Meadow Well	14.11.1982			

Percy Main	18. 6.1839	11. 8.1980	29. 4.1968	14.11.1982
Howdon-on-Tyne	18. 6.1839	11. 8.1980	7. 7.1964	14.11.1982
Hadrian Road	14.11.1982			
Wallsend	19. 6.1839	11. 8.1980	[see Carville]	14.11.1982
Walker Gate	19. 6.1839	11. 8.1980	14. 8.1967	14.11.1982
Chillingham Road M	14.11.1982			
Heaton	1. 7.1847	1. 4.1887		(re-sited)
Heaton	1. 4.1887	11. 8.1980		
Byker M	14.11.1982			
Manors M	14.11.1982			
Manors East	1. 7.1847			
Carliol Square	20. 6.1839	30. 8.1850		
Monument M	15.11.1981			
St James M	14.11.1982			

MANORS - PERCY MAIN (via RIVERSIDE)

Opened

1. 5.1879	Riverside Jn (Byker) - Percy Main West Jn (via Carville)

Closed to passengers 23. 7.1973

Closed to goods (Dates by which lines were taken out of use)

31. 5.1978	Carville Swan Hunter Siding - Percy Main West Jn
4.1987	St Peters Shepherds Scrap Siding - Carville Swan Hunter Siding
31. 3.1988	Riverside Jn - St Peters Shepherds Scrap Siding (last used 25.9.1987)

Stations	Opened	Closed (passengers)	Closed (goods)	
Byker	1.3.1901	5.4.1954	—	(opened unadvertised 1884)
St Peters	1.5.1879	23.7.1973	31.10.1966	
St Anthonys	1.5.1879	12.9.1960		
Walker	1.5.1879	23.7.1973	14. 8.1967	
Carville	1.5.1879	23.7.1973	11. 7.1966	('Wallsend' goods from 1913)
Point Pleasant	1.1.1902	23.7.1973		(opened unadvertised? 1879)
Willington Ouay	1.5.1879	23.7.1973	2.10.1967	

SOUTH GOSFORTH - PONTELAND - DARRAS HALL

Opened

1. 6.1905	South Gosforth - Ponteland
1.10.1913	Ponteland - Darras Hall
1921	Darras Hall - Kirkheaton Colliery (Wallridge Mineral Railway) (coal, also unofficial service for miners)

Closed (Passengers)

17.6.1929	South Gosforth - Ponteland - Darras Hall
1929	Darras Hall - Kirkheaton Colliery (unofficial service for miners)

Reopened (Passengers)

10. 5.1981	South Gosforth - Bank Foot
17.11.1991	Bank Foot - branch to Airport

Closed (Goods)

by 1947	Darras Hall -Kirkheaton Colliery
2. 8.1954	Darras Hall - Ponteland
14. 8.1967	Ponteland - Prestwick ICI Sidings
10. 4.1978	South Gosforth Jn - Gosforth West Jn
6. 3.1989	Prestwick ICI Sidings - South Gosforth

Stations	Opened	Closed (passengers)	Closed (goods)	Reopened (passengers)
West Gosforth	1. 6.1905	17. 6.1929	14. 8.1967	10. 5.1981
Regent Centre	10. 5.1981		(on site of West Gosforth)	
Wansbeck Road	10. 5.1981			
Coxlodge	1. 6.1905	17. 6.1929	6.12.1965	10. 5.1981
Fawdon	10. 5.1981		(on site of Coxlodge)	
Kingston Park	15. 9.1985			
Bank Foot	10. 5.1981		(on site of Kenton Bank)	
Kenton Bank	1. 6.1905	17. 6.1929	3. 1.1966	10. 5.1981
Callerton Parkway	17.11.1991		(site immediately south of Callerton)	
Callerton	1. 6.1905	17. 6.1929	6.12.1965	
Airport	17.11.1991			
Ponteland	1. 6.1905	17. 6.1929	14. 8.1967	
Darras Hall	1.10.1913	17. 6.1929	2. 8.1954	

TYNE COMMISSION QUAY BRANCH

Opened (unadvertised) -.2.1900   Known as Albert Edward Dock until 1920

Opened (advertised) 15. 6.1928   **Closed** 2.10.1939 **Reopened** -.11.1945

Closed 4. 5.1970

BLYTH & TYNE RAILWAY ROUTE TO PERCY MAIN / WHITLEY, ALSO SEATON SLUICE LINE.

Opened to passengers:

28. 8.1841	Seghill - Percy Main (separate station from N&NS)
1847	Blyth - Hartley - Dairy House - Seaton Sluice
3. 3.1847	Blyth - Hartley - Seghill
31.10.1860	Hartley - Whitley (Avenue Branch) - Tynemouth

Closed to passengers:

14. 5.1852	Hartley - Dairy House - Seaton Sluice
27. 6.1864	Holywell (late Backworth) - Percy Main
27. 6.1864	Hartley - Monkseaton (Whitley) (Avenue Branch)
For further dates to 1964 see under **Coast Circle.**	
2.10.1964	Backworth / Monkseaton - Hartley - Blyth / Newbiggin

	Opened	Closed (passengers)	Closed (goods)
Hartley	3. 3.1847	2.11.1964	9.12.1963
Seaton Delaval	3. 3.1847	2.11.1964	9.12.1963
Seghill	28. 8.1841	2.11.1964	9.12.1963
Backworth	28. 8.1841	27. 6.1864	7. 6.1965
Prospect Hill	28. 8.1841	27. 6.1864	
Percy Main	28. 8.1841	27. 6.1864	
The Avenue	31.10.1860	27. 6.1864	
Seaton Sluice	1847	14. 5.1852	

Notes

Unadvertised re-opening of Backworth Colliery Railway to Percy Main for miners' wives (known as the 'Jam Train') between 1914 and 1918.
Reopened by North Tyneside Steam Railway on 11.8.1991 between Percy Main and Middle Engine House (Stephenson Museum).

NEWCASTLE - PELAW AND SOUTH SHIELDS BRANCH

M = Metro station on new route

Opened

10 9.1834	Brockley Whins - South Shields (minerals only)
16. 4.1835	Brockley Whins - South Shields (passengers)
5. 1.1839	Redheugh - Oakwellgate
19. 6.1839	South Shields - Monkwearmouth
5. 9.1839	Oakwellgate - Cleadon Lane (later East Boldon)
1. 3.1872	Pelaw Junction - Hebburn - Tyne Dock

Closed

30. 8.1850	Branch to Greenesfield
5.1853	Branch to Redheugh
1. 3.1872	Brockley Whins - Tyne Dock (passengers)
1. 6.1981	Pelaw (North Jn) - South Shields (passengers)
1. 6.1981	Tyne Dock (Harton Jn) - South Shields (all traffic)

Metro openings and reopenings

15.11.1981	Haymarket - Heworth
24. 3.1984	Heworth - Pelaw (North Jn) - Tyne Dock (Harton Jn) Deviation from new Tyne Dock station - South Shields (via Chichester)

Stations	Opened	Closed (passengers)	Closed (goods)	Reopened
Redheugh	1. 3.1837	-. 8.1850		11.1852 to -.5.1853
Oakwellgate	5. 9.1839	2. 9.1844		
Greenesfield	15. 1.1839	30. 8.1850		
Gateshead East	18. 6.1844	23.11.1981		
(Gateshead West	1.12.1868	1.11.1965)		
Gateshead **M**	15.11.1981			
Gateshead Stadium **M**	15.11.1981			
Felling	5. 9.1839	18.11.1896		(new site to west)
Felling	18.11.1896	5.11.1979	2. 8.1965	15.11.1981
Heworth	5.11.1979			
Pelaw	5. 9.1839	by 1857		(new site 180 yd E)
Pelaw	by 1857	18.11.1896		(first site again)
Pelaw	18.11.1896	5.11.1979	4.10.1965	16. 9.1985
Hebburn	1. 3.1872	1. 6.1981	4.10.1965	24. 3.1984
Jarrow	1. 3.1872	1. 6.1981		24. 3.1984
Bede	24. 3.1984			
Tyne Dock	19. 6.1839	1. 6.1981		(new site)
Tyne Dock **M**	24. 3.1984			
High Shields	19. 6.1839	2. 6.1879		(new site 180 yd N)
High Shields	2. 6.1879	1. 6.1981		
Chichester **M**	24. 3.1984			
South Shields	16. 4.1835	19. 8.1844		
South Shields	19. 6.1839	17.12.1842		(new site; line extended)
South Shields	17.12.1842	2. 6.1879		(new site)
South Shields	2. 6.1879	1. 6.1981	31.3.1970	(new site)
South Shields	24. 3.1984			(100 yd S of previous sta)

SPRINGWELL - JARROW

Opened to passengers 5.9.1839   Closed to passengers 1.3.1872

SOUTH SHIELDS (Westoe Lane) - MARSDEN - WHITBURN COLLIERY

5.1879	Opened unofficially for miners to Whitburn Colliery
3.1885	Opened unofficially for general passenger traffic (for a short time only)
19. 3.1888	Became public railway from Westoe Lane to Marsden ($\frac{1}{2}$ mile north of Whitburn Colliery terminus)
c.1900	Marsden Cottage Halt (unadvertised) opened
c.1926	Marsden station closed. Public service extended to Whitburn Colliery
20.11.1953	Closed (passengers)
1968/69	Whitburn Colliery - South Shields (Mowbray Road) goods closed (Colliery closed 8.6.1968; line used by a railtour on 7.9.1968)
7.1969	Tracks removed; official closure date not known

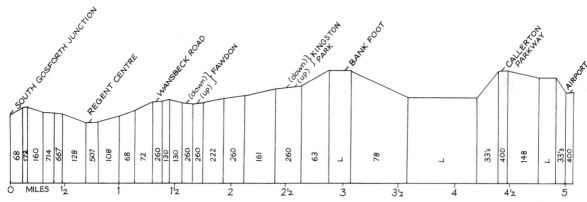

Gradients : South Gosforth to Airport : Tyne & Wear Metro.